Farming the Dust Bowl

LAWRENCE SVOBIDA

Farming
the Dust Bowl
A First-Hand Account from Kansas

LAWRENCE SVOBIDA

FOREWORD BY R. DOUGLAS HURT

UNIVERSITY PRESS OF KANSAS

DEDICATED

to the vast multitudes of homeless men and
women and children, who, being haunted by
famine, disease, and death, abandoned
everything, through sheer desperation, in
their bid for freedom from the everlasting
dust menace.

Foreword © 1986 by the University Press of Kansas
Copyright 1940 by The Caxton Printers, Ltd.; 1968 by Lawrence Svobida
All rights reserved

Originally published as *An Empire of Dust*. This edition appears by exclusive
arrangement with Caxton Printers.

Published by the University Press of Kansas (Lawrence, Kansas 66049), which was
organized by the Kansas Board of Regents and is operated and funded by Emporia
State University, Fort Hays State University, Kansas State University, Pittsburg
State University, the University of Kansas, and Wichita State University

Library of Congress Catalog Card Number: 86-80328
ISBN 0-7006-0289-5
ISBN 0-7006-0290-9 (pbk.)

Printed in the United States of America
5   4

CONTENTS

FOREWORD

*W*HAT *FOLLOWS* is the story of Lawrence Svobida, a Kansas wheat farmer who fought searing drought, wind, erosion, and economic hard times in the Dust Bowl. It is a vivid account by a farmer who pitted his physical strength, mental faculties, and financial resources against the environment as nature wreaked havoc across the southern Great Plains. Svobida's description of Dust Bowl agriculture is important not only because it accurately describes farming in that region but also because it is one of the few first-hand accounts that remain of the frightening and still haunting dust-laden decade of the 1930's. As such, it is a valuable record of the past.

When Lawrence Svobida came to Meade County, Kansas, in 1929, he was a young man from the western edge of the Corn Belt, who had a strong constitution and a burning desire to be a wheat farmer. The Meade County land, which his father owned, offered him the opportunity to prove himself, just as his strength and will had enabled him to excel in the Nebraska cornfields. He found the Kansas soil fertile and the future full of promise. Svobida, of course, did not realize that he had settled in a region that soon would be known as the Dust Bowl. He did not foresee that skill and perseverance would not be enough to ensure successful agriculture on the southern Great Plains or that Franklin Delano Roosevelt soon would offer a ''New Deal'' to farmers, thereby enabling them to remain on the land after personal finances and hope were almost gone.

Although Svobida arrived in southwestern Kansas in 1929, when the environment was on the verge of drastic change, the Dust Bowl had been in the making for nearly half a century. By the mid 1880's, farmers were settling the grasslands of the southern Great Plains, and by 1910, they had claimed nearly the entire region. Steel plows quickly broke the sod, grain drills efficiently planted seed, and binders and headers swiftly harvested the crops; wheat farming became the main agricultural activity. By the turn of the twentieth century, the days of the cattle kingdom had faded into the past, and steam engines had often replaced horses in front of the plow as well as powered threshing machines. The outbreak of a new European war in 1914 had also boosted wheat prices and encouraged farmers to expand production. Each acre of plowed sod, however, meant that less grass remained to hold the soil against the persistent winds. When high agricultural prices collapsed during the early 1920's, Meade County farmers and others like them on the southern Great Plains broke more sod for wheat than ever before to compensate for the economic loss. A new form of technology—the tractor—enabled farmers with speed and ease to plow the grasslands for planting wheat, and combines increasingly harvested the crop quickly before the grain could shrivel in the heads or be lost to bad weather. Few farmers, however, gave much thought to using this new technology to conserve the soil. Instead, the expansion of the wheat lands continued at a rapid pace. Between 1925 and 1931, wheat acreage doubled on the southern plains, and in some counties it expanded tenfold.

Throughout the twenties, wheat farmers on the southern Great Plains clung to the steering wheels of their tractors as these machines relentlessly lumbered across the land, pulling one-way disk plows. In the wake of the plows, the roots of the sod lay exposed to the wind and the sun. Five to six million acres of that newly broken sod were submarginal—that is, land not fit for cultivation given the current price of wheat. That land was easily windblown, and it should have been left in the protective hold of the grass. Yet across the southern plains, farmers plowed acre after acre and transformed rangeland to breadbasket. "My tractor," Svobida wrote, "roared day and night, and I was turning eighty acres every twenty-four hours, only stopping for servicing once every six hours." A hired man drove the tractor for a twelve-hour shift beginning at 6:00 A.M., and Svobida rode it throughout the night. The roar of the tractor was "music" to his ears.

As a result, wheat fields sprawled across the southern plains. Despite low prices, the region seemed to be a land of milk and honey. Where the newly turned sod lay black against the landscape, it turned green each autumn with the next wheat crop. When the golden stalks moved in waves with the wind before the sickle bar of the combines, wheat farmers were satisfied that by their labor they were making the land pay rich dividends.

Indeed, they wrung every possible bit of productivity from the soil. Although only 259,000 acres were suitable for wheat production in Meade County, Kansas, for example, farmers had seeded 288,000 acres to that crop by 1930. As long as the wheat grew, its fibrous root system held the soil against the persistent winds, and as long as the precipitation remained normal, all went well. The environment of the southern Great Plains, however, is harsh. Although agriculture there can generally be conducted with profit, the climatic pendulum swings back and forth. It has always done so. For Lawrence Svobida and others like him, it was about to swing in an ominous direction. When it did, their lives would change dramatically, and they would bear the scars of that experience for the rest of their lives.

By 1930, more than 50 percent of the rangeland in southwestern Kansas had been plowed for cultivation, primarily of wheat. When prolonged drought accompanies cultivation, however, the region's soil structure is easily broken down into small particles. The result is a fine, powder-dry soil which readily moves across the land with the slightest wind. In southwestern Kansas, for example, 68.5 percent of the soil is light silt loam. In Meade County, where Svobida farmed, 64.2 percent of the land is composed of silt loam, and an additional 14.9 percent is slightly heavier sandy loam. Thus, 80 percent of the soil is easily blown by the wind. Much of this land was submarginal; two-thirds of it should have been left in grass, rather than broken for wheat.

In 1931, with ample rainfall, these soils produced a record wheat crop. Before the year ended, however, drought had descended across the land. For the next two years, Meade County suffered an annual precipitation deficiency of five inches from the average of 19.92 inches. By August, 1934, Meade County was nearly twenty-one inches below normal over the previous three and one-half years. Other portions of the southern plains were even drier. Every inch of precipitation, however, is critical to agricultural survival in this region. When the rains ceased and the protective winter snows stopped falling, the wheat died, leaving the land exposed to the relentless winds. February, March, and April—the "blow months"—consistently have winds of the highest velocity, and by 1932 the soil was dry, pulverized, and easily lifted by the wind. Indeed, in the spring of 1932 the first dust storms swept over the southern Great Plains. As the soil drifted, more crops were ruined, which in turn exposed additional land to erosion. Wind erosion became a major problem, which steadily worsened.

Although the boundaries of the Dust Bowl cannot be drawn precisely, its general location encompassed an area of some 97 million acres in southeastern Colorado, northeastern New Mexico, southwestern Kansas, and the panhandles of both Texas and Oklahoma. The area measured roughly four hundred miles from north to south and three hundred miles from east to west, with the approximate center at Liberal in Seward County, near the southwestern corner of Kansas. Wind erosion was the most severe within a hundred-mile radius of that town, and neighboring Meade County to the east fell within the heart of the Dust Bowl. The outline of the Dust Bowl changed somewhat from year to year, depending upon precipitation. The area where wind erosion was the worst, known as the "blow area," never covered the entire 97 million acres of the Dust bowl that potentially were subject to severe wind erosion. The blow area, however, encompassed about 50 million acres by the mid 1930's and was concentrated largely in southwestern Kansas.

By that time, low prices, caused by overproduction, and crop failure, caused by drought, had exhausted the resources of wheat farmers in the southern plains. Many farmers could no longer afford to apply the appropriate soil-conservation techniques, and absentee, or "suitcase," farmers left their lands to the mercy of the winds. As the crops withered and the soil rose with the winds, the "black blizzards" became a household fear. These dust storms brought darkness at noon, stranded motorists and trains, filled the insides of houses with dust, and brought death to old and young alike from an illness that doctors diagnosed as "dust pneumonia."

The black blizzards tested the mettle of Dust Bowl residents. Spirits plunged when the dust clouds billowed overhead. In 1934, a mid-March dust storm in Meade County "did about everything but take the last hope of the people." Yet most residents stoically accepted their fate. This willingness to endure is exemplified by a Meade County woman who, during the black blizzard of April 14, 1935, the worst in memory, dragged her rocking chair into the middle of a room and sat down. She watched while the "dark brown mass" of soil pressed tightly against the window panes, where it hung like a curtain with no visible motion. Although she thought the end of the world was at hand, she was filled with a satisfying peace, because the tape along the window and door frames held out nearly every bit of dust and that was, she wrote, "a condition under which almost any housewife could have died happily."

As the dust of one year sifted into the next, most people prayed for rain, and churches held public prayer meetings for that purpose. While some believed the dust storms were a form of God's punishment for a sinful past, or at least Divine will, others took the storms in stride as being merely a prolonged aberration of generally good weather in normal times. Many residents, reflecting a staunch regional pride, made fun of the dust storms with a humor as dry as it was witty. Humor helped residents to cope, but it also showed their determination to adapt to the environment. This determination is nowhere more clearly illustrated than in the efforts of John L. McCarty, editor of the *Dalhart Texan*, who urged Dust Bowl residents to "grab a root and growl." He organized the Last Man's Club, membership in which was available to anyone who pledged to be the last one to leave the Dust Bowl. For McCarty and others like him, the southern Great Plains was a good place to live—only rain was needed to make it a perfect place to raise a family and to live in prosperity and tranquillity.

Not everyone, however, chose to stay and make a fight of it. Discouraged by persistent drought, drifting soil, ruined crops, broken health, dust-laden air, and lost dreams, some residents loaded their belongings into the family truck or car and left for an uncertain future elsewhere. Those who hit the highways, however, were not all headed for California, as John Steinbeck has led us to believe. Dust Bowl farmers frequently moved, but they usually went to the nearest town, instead of to the Pacific Coast. Nor did they alone make up the great "Okie" migration, epitomized in the heartbreaking photographs taken by Dorothea Lang and Arthur Rothstein. Between 1930 and 1935, for example, the population of Meade County decreased by only 3 percent. At that same time, no house in Meade stood vacant, and the county's two main villages, Plains and Fowler, gained population as farm workers, tenants, and the elderly moved from the farms to the towns to seek employment or to be closer to the relief offices. Although the population of Meade County dropped by 20 percent during the entire decade and although each departure represents a personal tragedy which statistics easily hide, the cumulative migration was not of sufficient size to label it a Dust Bowl exodus. Most Kansas wheat farmers simply had too much invested in their lands to leave, and the government helped them to stay. In 1935, for example, 545 Meade County farmers were either full- or part-time owners, while 331 farmers were tenants.

Certainly, many Dust Bowl farmers became discouraged, and some quickly left or resolutely accepted their fate. But Lawrence Svobida and others like him did not, and they worked hard to restore the land. The most knowledgeable and financially solvent farmers went into the blowing fields with their tractors hitched to listers, one-way disk plows, spring-tooth harrows, or chisels to turn over the blowing soil and create a rough, or furrowed, surface to slow or catch the moving soil. This strategy, however, lasted only a short time before it had to be repeated, and without accompanying moisture, the treatment further broke down the soil structure and made it more susceptible to wind erosion. With the financial and technical support of the Department of Agriculture's Soil Conservation Service and other federal agencies, the best Dust Bowl farmers also practiced strip cropping, to help slow the wind, anchor the soil, and prevent it from blowing. Strip cropping involved planting a close-growing, soil-holding crop, such as wheat, alternately with contoured strips of thickly growing crops, such as grain sorghum or sudan grass, both of which grew rapidly and provided a thick wind-resistant growth. They also created soil-conservation districts, built terraces, used contour plowing, reseeded parched grasslands, and planted more drought-resistant sorghum grain. Generally, Dust Bowl farmers were an optimistic and tenacious lot. Indeed, they were the best "next year" people in the world: next year the rains would come; next year the wheat would make a bountiful crop; next year the grass would grow and all would be well.

By the autumn of 1938, however, Svobida no longer was optimistic about these efforts. He had not harvested a profitable wheat crop since 1931, and he doubted that the Dust Bowl ever could be restored to productive agriculture. Indeed, Svobida was discouraged because soil conservation could be effective only if all farmers took the appropriate conservation measures to halt the "march of destruction." Svobida recognized, however, that "strict regulation" of farming practices would be required to achieve successful soil conservation. The government (he did not specify at which level) would need to provide legislation and enforce it in order to guarantee that all farmers would use their lands wisely to prevent wind erosion and thereby improve conditions in the Dust Bowl.

Svobida was not alone in looking for regulatory relief. Although Kansas and Texas, for example, had such legislation on the statute books, a group of Texas, Oklahoma, and Kansas farmers and businessmen met in Guymon, Oklahoma, in April, 1937, to discuss soil conservation. They resolved that the federal government should determine the boundaries of the Dust Bowl and declare martial law within it. Once that was accomplished, all cultivated land could then be forcibly subjected to the appropriate conservation measures. Some residents favored the creation of a federal bureau of

aridity, or Dust Bowl Authority, to supervise conservation and relief work in the region and to develop a
permanent soil-conservation program. This desire is
noteworthy because normally, such governance ran
absolutely contrary to the independent principles and
beliefs of most Dust Bowl farmers. Nothing came of this
resolution, but it indicates that the severity of Dust
Bowl conditions drove people to seek unusual solutions,
even if that meant increased governmental regulation of
their lives.

Although the resources of state governments were
limited and while no governmental agency imposed the
control that Svobida thought necessary to solve the
problem of wind erosion, the federal government did
provide a multiplicity of New Deal aid programs. In
1935, for example, the Soil Conservation Service provided demonstration areas and technical expertise to
support farmers who were trying to gain control of their
blowing lands through proper tillage and cropping pro-
cedures, such as listing, strip cropping, and reseeding of
grasslands. The Civilian Conservation Corps also established demonstration projects in the Dust Bowl. A host
of federal agencies, such as the Federal Emergency
Relief Administration (FERA), provided funds to finance
soil-conservation operations and to enable farmers to
purchase feed, seed, and fuel, as well as daily necessities, so that they could remain on the land until the
rains returned and they were able to bring the soil under
control. Indeed, more than 75 percent of the wheat
acreage in southwestern Kansas produced less than

three bushels per acre annually between 1933 and 1937; and 40 percent yielded less than one bushel per acre. As a result, in the Dust Bowl federal aid meant the difference between staying and leaving the farm.

No federal agency, however, was more important than the Agricultural Adjustment Administration (AAA), which Franklin Delano Roosevelt's "First Hundred Days" Congress created in the spring of 1933. The AAA, in part, paid farmers to reduce their production of certain surplus crops, such as wheat. Most Dust Bowl farmers participated in the AAA program, because they could not afford to do otherwise. Although they would have preferred to plant wheat from fence row to fence row and then pray for rain, they had no choice but to accept AAA checks if they wanted to remain on the land. With continued crop failures, they nearly were destitute, and indeed, AAA checks provided the major income for Dust Bowl farmers between 1933 and 1937.

In Meade County, where Svobida participated in the program, the AAA had provided more than $333,500 in agricultural income for wheat farmers by June, 1934. A second payment that year for acreage reductions brought an additional $135,000 to wheat farmers. Although few Dust Bowl farmers raised corn and hogs, payments for reduction of each brought nearly $28,000 to Meade County farmers by April, 1935. Dust Bowl farmers used this financial support to pay taxes and to cover living expenses. Without the AAA, the rate of failure and abandonment of farms would have been disastrous.

Cattlemen also received governmental aid. In mid May, 1934, the federal government created the Drought Relief Service (DRS), under the direction of the AAA, to purchase cattle in counties where drought and wind erosion were the most severe. Cattle in these "emergency" counties did not have adequate feed and water and were in great danger of dying. By late summer the AAA had declared that almost the entire Dust Bowl was an emergency area, thereby enabling cattlemen to sell selected livestock to the DRS. Federal purchases, however, obligated participating cattle producers to support a production-control program in the future.

In June, 1934, the first Dust Bowl cattle purchases in Meade County began. Officials destroyed and buried all cattle that were unsuitable for food and transferred all other purchased livestock to packing plants. The Federal Surplus Relief Corporation (FSRC) then distributed the canned beef to needy families nationwide. In the Sunflower State the FSRC authorized the Kansas Emergency Relief Committee (KERC) to receive the purchased cattle. At first most of these cattle were shipped to packers out of state. Later, however, the FERA authorized the KERC to contract locally with private packers and canners to process the meat. Ultimately, eighteen canning projects accounted for the slaughter of more than 102,000 head of KERC cattle to supply fresh beef for the state's relief program.

The Emergency Cattle Purchase Program enabled many stockmen to sell substantial numbers of cattle that would otherwise have perished from heat, starvation, and suffocation. It also enabled stockmen to cull inferior breeding animals and thereby improve their foundation herds. By mid August, 1934, Meade County cattlemen had received $79,000 in cattle payments. When the program ended in mid February, 1935, they had sold nearly 12,000 cattle to the federal government for more than $175,000. In Kansas, the Emergency Cattle Purchase Program removed 316,000 cattle from the parched grazing lands of the Dust Bowl and, at the same time, put $4.5 million in the pockets of stockmen during a time of dire need. The federal government also purchased 680,000 cattle from the drought area in other Dust Bowl states, at a cost of $8.6 million. Indeed, this program helped to prevent financial ruin among Dust Bowl cattlemen.

Dust Bowl farmers received other support as well. The Resettlement Administration (RA), which was created in April, 1935, provided loans to farmers who could not obtain credit elsewhere. These loans enabled them to purchase feed, seed, fertilizer, food, and clothing until precipitation and self-sufficiency returned. The Farm Security Administration (FSA), which replaced the RA in 1937, made similar loans to farmers who, under normal conditions, operated viable farms. The Rural Rehabilitation Corporation (RRC) also provided feed for livestock, and the AAA granted loans for feed and forage as well as payments for contour listing and for planting cover crops of grain sorghum. Moreover, the FSRC opened its grain reserves to Dust Bowl cattlemen.

This aid certainly did not make Dust bowl farmers rich, but it enabled them to maintain their operations until the dust settled, the rains resumed, and life returned to normal. Farmers in Meade County, for example, from 1931 through 1934, received more than $204,500 from the Farm Credit Administration for crop-production loans. In addition, between 1933 and 1937, when the first phase of the AAA ended, that agency paid Meade County farmers $1.8 million. By mid June, 1937, under a revamped AAA program which enabled farmers to collect funds for planting soil-conserving rather than surplus-producing crops, Meade County farmers received an additional $313,500. Between 1933 and 1937, Meade County farmers also garnered $1.8 million from the Federal Land Bank; $237,000 from the AAA in emergency crop loans; nearly $69,000 from the RRC; almost $47,000 from the Production Credit Association; and $19,000 from the RA to help them fight the triple plagues of drought, dust, and economic depression.

Most of the Meade County farm families who received some form of relief lived in the southern portion of the county, where the wind easily lifted the sandy loam soils and where wind erosion was the worst. Lawrence Svobida was among the 90 percent of Meade County farmers who accepted aid from the federal government. He also was among the 81 percent who received federal support of some sort for their wheat crops. Aid such as this enabled Meade County farmers, despite Dust Bowl conditions, to keep nearly 351,000 of 617,000 acres under cultivation by 1936. With 56.8

percent of the county in cropland and with 43.1 percent of the land, or 266,000 acres, in pasture, only 0.1 percent of the county was available for other purposes. Within this large agricultural area, however, 134,000 acres, or 21.7 percent of the land, was either lying fallow, idle, or abandoned. This was the acreage that provided much of the soil that was blown during the dust storms.

Townspeople, of course, needed aid too. In June, 1934, 319 households in Meade County were on relief, 89 percent of which had not been on those rolls prior to 1933. By 1937, county residents, most of whom lived in Meade, Fowler, and Plains, had received $91,000 from the Civil Works Administration; $77,000 from the Works Progress Administration; $279,000 from the FERA; and an undetermined amount from the Public Works Administration as well as several smaller grants from other sources. By 1937 the population of 6,858 had received more than $3 million in relief. While these figures appear large, even generous, this relief provided, over a span of four years, only $437 per person, or about $110 annually. Nevertheless, the magnitude and the variety of that aid was unprecedented. Certainly, the fortunes of the townsfolk were linked closely to those of the farmers. When the soil blew and the wheat harvest dropped to a mere 12 percent of the previous ten-year average and prices plummeted, residents in Meade County and other parts of the Dust Bowl were faced with ecological and economic problems of unprecedented magnitude. Taxes and mortgages went unpaid, public services declined, and some people left the Dust Bowl never to return.

Those who stayed on the farm, such as Lawrence Svobida, sought new lands to cultivate. The drought did not discourage them. Instead, ironically, it stimulated them to buy or rent all lands that were suitable for wheat production so that they might recover their losses from the previous years of failure. By so doing, of course, Meade County and other Dust Bowl farmers actually worked against the intent of the AAA. Instead of curtailing production, many wheat farmers signed AAA contracts, which obligated them to reduce production on their own lands, and then sought additional lands for planting. In this way they hedged their bets. If it rained, the good times would return. If it did not, at least they would receive some funds, which would enable them to maintain operation for another year. Moreover, few Dust Bowl farmers relied entirely on wheat. Although diversification was minimal, most raised some livestock and, like Svobida, feed grains. While diversification helped Dust Bowl farmers to remain on the land, only rain could restore prosperity. But little precipitation fell between 1932 and 1938. As a result, the wheat shriveled, and the grass turned a tawny brown. Thistles tumbled across the land.

While Dust Bowl farmers expanded their operations, diversified, or endured the best they could, waiting for the rains to return, the federal government also experimented with a plan to purchase submarginal land and return it to grass. The most severely wind-eroded lands, known as "nuisance lands" or "blow hazards," were to be turned into demonstration areas, where farmers could observe the best conservation methods. Eventually, those restored lands would be leased to farmers for grazing purposes under the watchful eye of the federal government. To achieve that goal, federal officials first identified the "problem" areas, where wind erosion was most severe, and developed a plan to purchase as much land as possible within that area. Then, government officials offered to buy the land and, if the owners agreed, took options to do so. Upon approval by the attorney general, the Treasury Department issued a check, and the sale was completed.

In the autumn of 1934 the federal government began to purchase submarginal land under the auspices of the AAA. At first, employees of the project furrowed the "blow lands" to catch the moving soil and to hold as much precipitation as possible. They planted drought-resistant crops, such as black amber cane and sudan grass, to reduce the wind velocity at ground level and to hold the blowing soil. Government workers also re-seeded plowed fields and barren pastures to restore the range land and thereby to protect the soil from further erosion. By the time the land-use purchase program ended in 1943, it had been administered by the RA, the FSA, and the Soil Conservation Service. Over the course of nine years, the federal government acquired several hundred thousand acres within the Dust Bowl. The program, however, always suffered from insufficient funds and bureaucratic delays, and it was never successful in buying all of the lands that it required or desired. Some landowners objected to the program, because property valuations were low and because purchase payments were slow to arrive. Even so, most Dust Bowl residents supported the federal government's unprecedented experiment in state planning. Today, these land-use projects remain landmarks of the Dust Bowl experience. Since 1960 they have been designated as National Grasslands—Cimarron in Kansas, Comanche in Colorado, Kiowa in New Mexico, and Rita Blanca in the Oklahoma and Texas panhandles.

While the land-use projects were being developed during the spring of 1938, the rains began to return, and the dust storms decreased in number and diminished in intensity. In 1938, thanks to the best subsoil moisture in many places since 1931, Dust Bowl farmers harvested a modest wheat crop. Compared to the previous years, however, it seemed like a bountiful harvest. Agriculture improved still further in 1939, when precipitation returned to near normal and the menace of wind erosion ended. The wheat crop flourished, and the harvest that year was the best since 1932. Optimism once again prevailed, and one Dust Bowl editor proclaimed that the region had become a "horn of plenty." Land values soared, tripling in some areas. Moreover, the new war in Europe caused wheat prices to rise and the market to expand. By 1940 the black blizzards had gone, and the residents resolutely looked to a brighter future, convinced that the purgatory of the past was behind them.

Indeed, the long-awaited better days seemed to be at hand. In 1940, Meade County farmers harvested

169,000 acres of cropland, compared to 117,000 acres
six years before, with a crop value of $665,000. The
1940 wheat crop yielded 778,800 bushels, valued at
nearly $522,000, from 141,530 acres, in comparison to
the 1934 yield of 599,000 bushels, valued at $503,000,
from 104,000 acres. Between 1935 and 1940, Meade
County farms also grew in size, as some farmers sold
out and the more prosperous agriculturists expanded
their holdings. During that time the average Meade
County farm increased in size from 675.5 to 748.9
acres, while the number of farms decreased from 883 to
750. The average value of Meade County farms also
increased from $12,823 in 1935 to $14,173 in 1940,
although that was still substantially below the $21,578
average in 1930.

Although most Dust Bowl farmers did not leave the
region, Lawrence Svobida ultimately chose to do so. In
1939, after the failure of seven wheat crops in eight
years, he was thoroughly discouraged. Moreover, his
health, as well as his spirit, was broken. Although he
had fought tenaciously against the persistent drought,
searing heat, and blowing dust, often far better than less
skillful or conscientious farmers, he gave up and moved
elsewhere. Perhaps he went to Idaho, where this
account of his Dust Bowl experiences was first published in 1940. He had, by then, become convinced that
the Dust Bowl was creating a "new" Great American
Desert. Svobida was not alone in that belief. Others saw
the making of a "forbidding desert" that would be
"similar to sands that once knew the footprints of the

Queen of Sheba.'' They speculated that in time it would cover the Great Plains and that many eastern cities would have a fate similar to the ancient civilizations in North Africa and the Middle East.

Svobida's chronicle of his life in the Dust Bowl is clearly written, although he did not write objectively, as he professed to do. Perhaps only a saint could have after experiencing so many heartbreaking failures. In reading his story, we see him being foiled at every turn. Like a modern-day Job, he suffered from drought, dust, and other calamities. The all-pervading influence of a hostile environment battered him constantly and ruined his crops. Certainly, life in the Dust Bowl, particularly for the farmer, was sufficiently difficult to blacken the heart of the most resolute citizens of the southern plains. But every day was not darkened by a dust cloud, parched by the sun, or blown by the wind. For the most part the dust storms came during the early spring, and blue skies and occasional light rain prevailed during the remainder of the year. Indeed, the sun scorched a thirsty land, drought continued for nearly a decade, and the dust storms loomed in everyone's mind, if not on the horizon, but most Dust Bowl residents fought back with a psychological and physical stamina based on humor, religion, and government aid.

Despite Svobida's pessimism, his story is vivid and remarkably complete. We learn that not all Dust Bowl farmers were not bad soil conservationists. We see the best methods being used to catch the soil and prevent it from moving and drifting across the land. We under-

stand the salvation of government aid and its obligations, as well as the concerns and worries of Dust Bowl
farmers. Thus, Svobida's accurate history is as important as it is absorbing. It is a chronicle that will make
anyone understand the dangers of overexpansion and
agricultural carelessness in the southern plains.

With the return of normal precipitation and high
wartime prices, however, agricultural expansion continued in the southern plains during the 1940's, more
sod was broken, and much of that newly cultivated land
was submarginal. Some authorities warned farmers
about past dangers, but the advice was not heeded.
Then, by the end of that decade, drought had returned
and with it the dust storms. During the early 1950's, the
drought area expanded far beyond the boundaries of the
old Dust Bowl. It stretched from southwestern Texas
to the Nebraska panhandle and from the Rocky Mountains in Colorado and New Mexico to western Kansas
and Oklahoma. Once again, soil drifted in fields, along
fence rows, and into towns. As the dust storms halted
traffic and interrupted daily life, farmers went into their
fields to plow furrows across the path of the prevailing
winds to slow and catch the moving soil. They had not
entirely forgotten the conservation lessons of the past,
and without facing an economic depression, most were
financially able to meet emergency tillage expenses.
Moreover, the federal government again came to the
aid of the drought-stricken, dust-laden farmers. The
United States Department of Agriculture quickly provided $15 million for emergency tillage. The Commodity

Credit Corporation supplied livestock feed at below market prices, and the Agriculture Department provided funds to help farmers pay transportation costs to ship hay into the region by railroad. The Farmers Home Administration also furnished loans for feed and seed, and other programs provided funds to help meet the costs of livestock raising, emergency tillage, and operating expenses.

By the spring of 1957 the drought had broken, and the dust had settled. Farmers were now more diversified than ever before, thanks to sorghum grains and irrigation. They no longer relied solely on wheat for their livelihoods, and if that crop failed, they would not immediately plunge into financial ruin. Moreover, Dust Bowl farmers had greatly expanded their irrigation systems since the 1930's. During the drought of the 1950's, southwestern Kansas farmers turned to irrigation to ensure crop harvests. At that same time, irrigation systems became more convenient and, during the 1960's, more affordable. Irrigation not only boosted harvests in the Kansas Dust Bowl, it also enabled substantial crop diversification and expansion of the livestock industry, particularly feeder cattle. With irrigation, farmers could safely plant corn where this crop would have been impossible to grow without it. By the early 1970's, irrigated corn had replaced dry-land grain sorghum in many western Kansas fields, and corn yields reached more than two hundred bushels per acre. Thus, irrigation began to change the look of the land.

Irrigation has also brought potential problems. The Ogallala Aquifer, for example, provides most of the ground-water supply for farmers in western Kansas, but its recharge rate is far slower than the rate of withdrawal. The recharge rate varies from one-fourth inch annually in southwestern Kansas to six inches annually in the east-central portion of the state. Because irrigation is heavy in southwestern Kansas and because the area receives only between sixteen and twenty inches of precipitation annually, water mining is becoming an increasingly serious problem. In some parts of Grant and Stanton counties the water table declined one hundred feet between 1939 and 1965, and drops of one to three feet annually are now common in sections throughout the old Dust Bowl. As a result, farmers must drill wells several hundred feet deep in southwestern Kansas to reach the life-giving water. Consequently, where farmers rely upon irrigation for more than crop insurance, the depletion of the ground-water supply eventually could force them to revert to supplementary irrigation or dry-land agriculture. Future energy costs may prove to be a limiting feature as well. Moreover, the brief periods of drought and blowing dust during the 1960's and 1970's clearly indicate the tenuous environmental balance in the southern plains, even with irrigation.

Still, Svobida's bleak prediction for the Dust Bowl has not been realized, and he would, no doubt, be pleased that his forecast of a new Great American Desert was incorrect. He loved the land and had a consuming desire to make it productive. Today, a half-century after the worst black blizzards rolled over the Dust Bowl, agriculture thrives in the region, despite the persistent problems of overproduction, low prices, and inadequate markets. In many respects the problems of the past remain. Yet the most serious—wind erosion—has been largely controlled. As a result, by the early 1980's, Meade County farmers produced nearly 3,862,000 bushels of wheat from 125,000 acres, and they used more than 1,000 tractors and 364 combines, in addition to custom cutters, to make their labors easier. They also grazed more than 46,000 head of cattle. Overall, Meade County farmers tended 339,000 acres of cropland and 256,000 acres of pasture, nearly the same acreage as that used in 1930. The average Meade County farm, however, has changed significantly. By the early 1980's, it had nearly doubled, to 1,214 acres. And the land was now valued at $509 per acre, up substantially from the value of $18.98 per acre in 1935. Despite the tremendous increase in land values, however, Meade County farmers were still relying on the federal government for assistance in a variety of programs. Loans from the Commodity Credit Corporation alone totaled $7,652,000 in 1982, and more than 150 farmers also participated in a federal diversion program whereby they were paid to set nearly 14,000 acres aside—that is, to cease from planting it.

Today, the wind still blows in the region of the Dust Bowl, and when it is combined with drought and inadequate vegetation, whether grass or wheat, the ingredients are present for a dust storm. This phenomenon will continue until man learns to control the climate or until he runs out of irrigation water to compensate for the harsh environment. Yet the environment of the southern Great Plains will not mandate a return of the Dust Bowl as long as the lessons of the past are not forgotten. And to ensure that remembrance, some congressmen from the Dust Bowl and other Great Plains states supported a "Sodbuster bill" during the early 1980s. This legislation, which Congress approved as part of the Food Security Act of 1985, barred federal benefits, such as price supports, crop insurance, and various loans, to farmers who plow the highly erodible grasslands that remain. This sentiment reflects Svobida's belief that strict enforcement of soil conservation would be necessary to bring the wind-eroded lands under control. Although the outcome of this agricultural regulation remains uncertain, Meade County today is not unlike Lawrence Svobida found it in 1929. For many farmers, who have the optimism he had fifty years earlier, the soil is still fertile, and the future remains full of promise.

R. Douglas Hurt
The State Historical Society of Missouri

PREFACE

*M*UCH has been written about the Dust Bowl, but the authors have been, for the most part, outsiders. If they have been residents of the Great Plains region, they have been dwellers in the towns. Both have taken an objective view of the farmers who have been fighting in the front-line trenches, putting in crop after crop, year after year, only to see each crop in turn destroyed by the elements.

As one of these farmers I have been fighting a losing battle for over nine years, giving freely of youth, strength, and exceptional stamina, and even recklessly drawing on the future by undermining a robust constitution. From my experience I have written a true, inside story of the plight of the average farmer in the Dust Bowl, relating facts without malice or prejudice against this great region. I have not exhibited the restraint shown by prominent citizens who are members of chambers of commerce, and who have a cautious eye on the tourist trade.

When an area extending over the greater part of ten states is rapidly becoming depopulated and appears doomed to become, in drear reality, the

"Great American Desert" shown on early maps and so described by writers until less than eighty years ago, then the time has passed when this story should be held back because of the reluctance of a few people who see in its telling a disadvantage to their own material interests. Surely the forced abandonment of thousands of farms, the reduction of once prosperous communities to the status of ghost towns, and the impoverishment of hundreds of thousands of people are events of national importance worthy of being recorded.

INTRODUCTION

FEW people realize that the Dust Bowl in the United States extends from the Canadian line to central west Texas, covering the entire western areas of Oklahoma, Kansas, Nebraska, North Dakota, and South Dakota, with extensive portions of Montana, Wyoming, Colorado, and New Mexico. It is almost coextensive with the region known as the Great Plains, the same region where once the buffalo roamed in great herds, some numbering half a million individuals, aggregating an estimated total of some twelve million animals. Here, too, were the hunting grounds of the Plains Indians, the boldest and most warlike tribes the white man ever had to deal with on this continent.

Certain hardy and nutritious grasses, notably the grama and buffalo grasses, were the basis of life on the Great Plains. They sustained the millions of buffalo and antelope, which in turn sustained the wolves, the coyotes, and the Indians; and these same grasses were later the basis of the cattle kingdom of the white man, originating in Texas and spreading ever northward to the Canadian border and beyond.

Railroads with land grants to dispose of, states with land scrip to sell, the Federal Government with its homestead policy, speculators, and barbed wire, all combined to restrict and eventually to abolish most of the free range, but cattle and horse raising continued to be the most important industry over a large part of the Great Plains until the 1920's.

Here had been overgrazing before the coming of the settlers and the invasion of barbed wire, but the death knell of the Plains was sounded and the birth of the Great American Desert was inaugurated with the introduction and rapid improvement of power farming. Tractors and combines made of the Great Plains region a new wheat empire, but in doing so they disturbed nature's balance, and nature is taking revenge.

From newspaper stories, garbled from Government reports, it is easy to get an impression of the Dust Bowl farmers as an impoverished lot of submarginal people eking out a miserable existence on submarginal land. On the contrary, most of these people are of the finest American stock, the descendants of pioneers from New England, descendants of cattlemen, and newcomers from Illinois, Indiana, Ohio, Iowa, eastern Kansas, and Nebraska. When the sod was broken to the plow on a large scale, the job called for capital, and capital was poured in without stint. So also were ambition, intelligence, energy, and enthusiasm.

That these people are being driven from farms and towns, that today tens of thousands are wandering, homeless, through California, Oregon, Washington, and Idaho, referred to, often contemptuously, as "Migs" and "Gypsies," is a national tragedy.

Since Meade County, Kansas, has been the scene of my own activities for the better part of a decade, I have made an intimate study of its history. Three times in less than seventy years the western part of Kansas has been settled and, in turn, vacated. Back in 1870, homesteaders settled along the river and creek bottoms. These sturdy, stout-hearted pioneers asked only a living from one year to another, with the opportuniy to acquire by a lifetime of hard work a surplus sufficient to secure a modest independence for their declining years. They found it hard sledding from the beginning, but most of them managed to stick it out until the spring of 1873, when they suffered a grasshopper invasion.

These pests descended in clouds so thick that they obstructed the view of the sun. They ate the green wheat, corn, cane, and grass, leaving the ground bare. They ate everything that had made existence possible for the early settlers—even the leaves and bark from the trees—and the entire population was forced to vacate, or face starvation for themselves and their livestock. From one observer we have the picture of a settler with a horse and a cow hitched to his wagon to furnish the pulling power to get away; while another pioneer with a sense of humor that persisted in adversity is reported to have painted on the side of his covered wagon, "In God We Trust—In Kansas We Bust."

The land that had been broken to the plow all went back to grass, and it was ten or twelve years before anyone ventured out here again to try to wrest a living from the soil. By 1886-87, however, all the land had once more been taken up, with a homesteader on almost every quarter section of land. Some brought wives and children, but the majority of the homesteaders were bachelors. Usually four single men would co-operate, each filing on the regulation quarter section of 160 acres, but pooling their resources so far as improvements were concerned. In the center of the section where their four quarters cornered, they would build a sod house on one quarter, erect stables on two others, and dig a well on the fourth quarter, which was in itself quite an undertaking with water often 140 feet below the surface. Besides being the most practical way to prove up under the homestead law, this practice was more companionable than that of each homesteader's living a dreary, lonely existence by himself.

As a rule, each settler broke out from twenty to forty acres, sufficient to provide a living under normal conditions.

In 1899, a severe drouth proved almost as disastrous as the earlier grasshopper plague had been. The farmers seeded their wheat in dry ground, and no moisture fell throughout the fall, winter, and spring. With no prospect of a crop, most of the inhabitants packed up and left. The following fall, when rain came, the wheat that had lain in the soil for a whole year sprouted and came up, and, with a few favoring rains in the spring, this wheat grew to maturity, yielding from twenty to twenty-five bushels to the acre. The few farmers who had remained harvested their own wheat, then moved their headers to surrounding fields belonging to those who had left the region. The latter learned nothing about the unexpected harvest.

Shortly after the turn of the century, people gradually drifted in once more, and from that period to the present many have come and gone, lingering long enough to spin the wheel of fortune in the game of chance known as wheat farming. Some were poor when they came, others wealthy; most of them, after weathering one, two, or even three crop failures, eventually lost everything they possessed.

One of the minor disasters of later years was the grasshopper invasion of 1919, a year that promised one of the best crops ever produced in the region, until the 'hoppers came. The lucky few who saved their crops that year were those who cut their wheat with binders while it was still a trifle green. In those days the majority still used headers, which required the grain to be harvested when dead ripe. The grasshoppers came from the south in their millions, and within twenty-four hours the standing crops were ruined. Grain that had promised to yield thirty bushels to the acre now yielded two or three bushels. The grasshoppers ate the straw three or four inches below the heads, which, consequently, fell to the ground. The insects craved something in the straw and did not molest the grain in the heads. That simply rotted on the ground.

At that time I saw pitchforks that had been left on partly finished stacks during the noon hour with the handles so pitted by the chewing of the 'hoppers that they had to be replaced before the implements could be used.

High winds in the Great Plains region are as normal as one year's following another. The usual windy season includes February, March, and April, during which period stiff gales occur two or three times a week, usually coming from a northerly direction at a velocity of thirty to forty miles an hour. They come up at any time of the day or night, and commonly last ten or twelve hours, though I have known them to persist for a much longer period, up to one hundred hours of continuous blowing. Particularly in recent years, these gales have invariably carried an immense amount of dust, so that breathing becomes extremely difficult during the height of a storm, and visibility is reduced to about a quarter of a mile, and sometimes to almost nothing.

History reveals that early caravans that crossed this territory a hundred years ago sometimes encountered dust storms during which visibility was reduced to as low as one hundred yards; but there is no report of general blowing of the land at that time. There occurred dry eras during which the wind might gain a toehold in the soil where it was light and poorly anchored by a thin covering of grass. Depressions were blown out, varying in size from small areas five yards or so in diameter to those that might embrace several acres. Within a few years all such depressions had become recarpeted with buffalo grass, and today they form sloughs and lagoons. Ten to fifty of them can be observed within ten miles of travel. They are commonly known as "buffalo wallows," from an erroneous belief which many people still hold that they were trampled out by the huge herds of bison that formerly made their home on the Great Plains.

The fact is that as long as the grass remained the Great Plains retained the power of recuperation. The winds blew, but the land did not, except to a limited extent in the dry eras. Only when the ground itself began to move with the wind was a desert born.

A few years ago Kansas was called "the breadbasket of the nation." It normally produced a fourth of the wheat supply. While only a limited portion of this western area was under cultivation and nearly all of it was covered with buffalo grass, it had supported thousands of herds of horses and cattle, and these grew sleek and fat. With the introduction of the more successful and more dependable tractors in later years, and the harvesting of two bumper crops in succession in the years 1928 and 1929, a great impetus was given to wheat farming in the region. These crops yielded from twenty-five to fifty bushels to the acre, some land producing even sixty bushels, so the farmers saw a golden opportunity. They disposed of their livestock, receiving a fair price for cattle, selling horses for any price they could get, and took up the raising of wheat on an extensive scale.

With more and more of the rolling prairie broken to the plow and drilled to wheat, the market sagged to sixty-five cents in 1930, then to the unbelievably low figure of twenty-five cents in 1931. This price was below the cost of production, and many of the farmers were forced into bankruptcy.

This might have been only a temporary setback to the region as a whole, but the winds began to attack the soil which was no longer anchored by the grass roots. From this came the black clouds of dust that blot out the sun, cross half a continent, and travel far out to sea. From this arose the Dust Bowl that is the new Great American Desert!

I HARVEST A WHEAT CROP

FIRED with the ambition to become a wheat farmer, I came to Meade County, Kansas, in 1929, at the enthusiastic age of twenty-one.

Life had run in pleasant channels in eastern Nebraska, where I was born. While my parents were not wealthy, they were prosperous enough so that I might have taken up any business or profession that appealed to me. As a matter of fact, from the time I was in knee pants my one and only ambition had been to be a farmer. Nature called to me, and I wanted to work close to her. Where one may see the glorious sun rise and set; where green, growing vegetation thrives; where birds warble and chirp merrily through life; where the air is clean, pure, and fresh—that was where I wanted to live and work.

Long before my own start in Kansas, I knew what farm work meant. At the age of nineteen, I had won local recognition as a champion corn shucker, not in organized contests, but working day after day in the field. At this work, which requires speed and stamina, I was superior to all others in the community. My motto was, "Never defeated," and I had made it good. I had husked

as much corn as any two other men together in
that community. I had been the only one to pile
enough corn in half a day's work to stop a team.
Not only did I bring one team to a standstill, but
two different teams the same day, one in the
morning and the other in the afternoon. These
were replaced by a third team of bigger, more
powerful horses, and even these had to exert their
utmost strength to pull out my fifty-bushel loads
every half day, with the wagon sunk halfway to
the axles in the loose, sandy soil.

At that I didn't reach the peak of my speed,
stamina, and skill at shucking corn until the following year, when I was twenty and demonstrated my ability in an Eastern corn state.

When I came to Meade County it was to take
over land that my father had owned for a quarter
of a century. This southwestern part of Kansas
has been exclusively a wheat belt for a number
of years. Because of its affinity to the native
grasses, wheat will grow where all other crops
fail. Here the land is practically level. For miles
and miles in any direction nothing obstructs the
distant horizon. Here in the past many fortunes
have been won and lost.

Power farming machinery is used: powerful
tractors with big ten-foot plows and multiple
hitched drills get over the ground quickly. It requires five thousand dollars for the necessary
equipment to raise and harvest a crop. A quarter

of land consists of 160 acres and the average farmer handles from four to six quarters, though there are a few men farming up to as high as six thousand acres.

My first year in Meade County was not auspicious. Three months after I had taken possession of my farm, I found myself in a hospital, unable to eat, sleep, or talk. I had already reached that condition, beyond the ability to work, before I went to see a doctor. He diagnosed my case as a throat infection and ordered me to bed. Sleep seemed to be the first essential, so a nurse, acting under the doctor's orders, gave me the necessary medicine. I slept. For forty hours I slept, interrupted only at mealtimes, when the nurse would tempt me with food I would try to eat. Outside the hospital it was rumored that I was dead, and I came near to confirming the rumor; and though the throat infection healed without an operation's being necessary, it was a long time before I could get back to the work of preparing my land for a wheat crop.

Nevertheless, I put in my first wheat crop that fall. Throughout the winter and spring, snow and rain fell in season, and the outlook was splendid. The crop promised to be a fine one, and I saw myself embarked on a career of my fondest preference.

I believe any man must see beauty in mile upon mile of level land where the wheat, waist high, sways to the slightest breeze and is turning a golden yellow under a flaming July sun. To me it

was breath-taking, the most beautiful scene in all
the world; and hundreds of acres of that wheat was
mine, representing the reward of labor, ambition,
and enterprise.

Business matters called me to another state, and
I went lightheartedly, but regretfully too, because
I wanted to watch my wheat reach its full maturity and the time of harvest. When I returned
I was filled with the joy of anticipation. I was
eager to see again the beautiful sight that meant
so much to me; and what I saw filled me with
amazement and sorrow. Hail had swept across
my land to beat down and destroy a large part of
my crop. The beauty was gone, leaving a wide
path of desolation through my fields; but on taking
stock, I found that I still had a lot of fine wheat—
enough so that I still might consider my first year
of operation as a wheat farmer a successful year.

The following day came calamity. Another hailstorm struck, and when it had passed the balance
of my crop lay ruined. Each of these storms swept
over a strip of land some seven miles long. They
were at different angles of direction, but both hit
my place, as though a malign fate had sought to
frustrate my efforts and my ambition. The disaster left me so blue and sick I could neither eat nor
sleep for several days.

After a time I was able to review what had
happened more dispassionately, and I saw that I
had taken at least one unnecessary gamble, so per-

haps Fate was not entirely at fault. I had had a small fortune within my grasp, and had let it slip through my hands. Most of it would have been saved to me if I had protected my crop with hail insurance. That was one mistake I would not make again. My next crop would be insured against that form of calamity.

As it was, instead of entering upon the joyous task of harvesting a big cash crop, I had to set myself to the task of cleaning up the mess the storms had left. I burned over my fields to get rid of the straw and what wheat was exposed above the ground. Then volunteer wheat kept coming up persistently, and this type of crop has to be destroyed because it never makes a uniform stand. Where it is too thick the first dry spell will kill it out. If too much rain penetrates, the weeds get ahead of the wheat in the thin spots. I had to plow the ground three times in order to get this situation under control.

Further to delay my work, the rains, commencing in September, continued through October and November with only occasional breaks. There was only a day, or possibly two, each week when the soil was dry enough to permit seeding, and all through my fields the sloughs were filled with water and were treacherously muddy at the edges. I had to pull around these sloughs, and now and then I would crowd in too close, though I would never know it until the tractor wheels started spinning and quickly dug themselves in to the axles. That meant the use of log chains to get the engine out on firmer soil, and then full power and all the traction I could get to yank the drills out of the mire. The task seemed an endless one and had become a nightmare to me before I finally finished drilling my seed by the last of October.

My second crop was in, and I watched it with anxiety, and it continued to make good progress until the freezing weather came in December. I felt that I had every reason to expect it to winter well, and I was not disappointed. By the first of March the weather had moderated, and when the ground thawed out and permitted the green vegetation to start, no one looking over the expansive land carpeted with green could have thought of this as desert country. It was a land of young growing things that gave rich promise of a bountiful harvest.

Then came the usual seesaw of promise and threat which ever faces the farmer. One morning in the latter part of March rain began, and by evening three inches of water had fallen. Towards night the temperature dropped, and the rain turned to snow. A driving wind was transformed into a raging blizzard that lasted all night.

That blizzard will long be remembered in western Kansas. Before it started there were still a few cattle raisers in the region, but the storm wiped them out. During the day the stock continued to graze contentedly on the range. The blizzard came with the darkness, and the ranchers were helpless to get their animals to shelter. Cattle drifted for miles with the storm, only to fall at last from exhaustion.

Desolate was the scene revealed when the storm lifted. Cattle had huddled in fence corners, by trees, in ditches, behind steep banks, any place that had seemed to offer shelter against the freezing onslaught of the gale. They were all dead. Scores of animals still stood knee deep in mud and slush that had frozen solid about their limbs, and they, too, were frozen stiff. One cattleman faced a loss that was staggering. An entire herd of eight hundred had blundered into a lake, and perished there. With the return of warm weather a week later the health officials ordered the owner to remove and bury the water-soaked, swelled, decaying carcasses. It required a strong will and a stronger stomach to comply with that order.

A mortgage company which held liens on a lot of the stock in the region had an appraiser checking up in the field for three months after the blizzard, but only rotting skeletons were left to check.

There was no damage to my wheat to be anticipated from a storm so early in the year, but we headed into a dry spell in April, and the growing crop suffered through many anxious days. Dry weather continued, and it looked as if I was going to lose again. This time I carried hail insurance, but I had no protection against drouth. In the middle of May rain came just in the nick of time to revive my crop, and once again I looked forward to a successful harvest.

Harvesting that crop was a thrill to me. The roar of the laboring motors and the whine of the combine were music in my ears. Day after day, from early morn until dark, toil was incessant, for time meant money. The combine was kept crowded to its fullest capacity, and every working minute was accounted for, because no one knew when a hailstorm might come up or a heavy rain strike to beat the ripe wheat flat upon the ground.

For the busy harvest season I had employed two men, and the wife of one of them kept house and did the cooking; but I was the one who had most at stake and I could not expect my employees to keep up the pace I set for myself. Just the job of keeping my tractor and combine in condition, with the necessary greasing and minor repairs, took from two to three of the early hours each morning, before the machines started rolling. I was six feet, one, in height, and weighed at that time one hundred and eighty pounds. When I found youth, physical strength, and surplus vitality not enough to keep up the pace I had set, I drew freely upon a strong constitution, and kept going from eighteen to twenty hours a day.

I was sustained by the elation of success. My fields were yielding from fifteen to thirty-five

The author's place in Meade County, Kansas, at its best.

Before the dust storms the Great Plains were a smiling land.

Horse raising was formerly a principal industry.

The land once flourished and cattle grew fat on the rich forage.

Multiple-hitched plows speeded the work in Kansas wheat fields.

New machinery and ripe grain—a wheat-field scene before the
years of dust and desolation.

Typical view of farm land that has begun to blow.

bushels to the acre, and I had hundreds of acres in wheat. Here was a golden harvest of grain that would justify my two years of labor. Once again I had a small fortune in my hands, and I had fully justified my ambition to be a farmer.

Alas! Wheat farming is always a gamble, and what actually happened to me that year illustrates what I mean. The slogan, "Kansas grows the best wheat in the world," is only justified by the fact that the wheat grown in Meade County, and in Gray County, adjoining to the north, is higher in protein content than any similar grain anywhere in the world. Because of the higher protein content it commands ten cents a bushel above the average market price; and if it hadn't been for that extra ten cents, I would have lost money on my 1931 crop. The bottom dropped out of the market that year, and at thirty to thirty-five cents a bushel for my wheat I barely cleared my expenses.

With a meager return for my two years of hard work, and no return at all on my investment, I still felt encouraged. I had proved that I could farm successfully and that my Meade County land could produce splendid crops of the finest quality wheat. There would be other good crop years. Surely, next time my wheat and my neighbors' wheat would bring a price that would set us all on top of the world.

CHAPTER II

THE LAND BEGINS TO BLOW

T̃HE DUST BOWL is not the creation of a day, nor yet of a single year, of drouth. That is why many wheat farmers are coming to the belief that it may already have become established beyond the knowledge and skill of all the Government conservation experts to restore the wasted land, or even to check seriously the processes of destruction now in operation in the Great Plains.

High winds in the early part of the year have always been normal to the region, but no dweller therein gave them a second thought until the land itself began to blow. By that time it was already too late to do much about it.

Our section of the Great Plains had enjoyed several good crop years in succession—1928, 1929, 1930, and 1931. But in 1929 and 1930 the land was already blowing in the Dakotas, and farmers there were abandoning their farms and leaving the region.

Most of our winds are from the northward, and when the land is blowing the effects are not confined. The dirt blown from the land in swirling clouds of dust covers the land adjacent to the blowing area. Soon that too is blowing; and thus the dust blight spreads like a contagion over the countryside.

Despite the miserably poor price received for my 1931 crop, the volume of that crop kept my courage high as I tackled the job of preparing my fields for another seeding. My tractor roared day and night, and I was turning eighty acres every twenty-four hours, only stopping for servicing once every six hours. I had a man driving from six in the morning until six in the evening. Then I would drive the laboring brute throughout the entire night.

Any wheat farmer will tell you that driving a tractor is a dangerous job during the hours between 3:00 A. M. and daylight, when you are likely to be working on the borderland of sleep. Often I could hardly keep my eyes open, and when I would doze off for a few seconds, only an instinctive but vicelike grip on the steering wheel kept me from falling and being ground to pieces under the plow. Many a man has met his death that way, but I was lucky; and I was getting my work done.

Perhaps I would have done better to save my labor, but I had lost my first crop from hail. The reward from my second effort had only cleared expenses, so I still had to make good as a wheat farmer. I come from a stubborn breed. First hail, then a bottomless wheat market had left me undismayed. I did not yet know that the dry era had commenced and that the spring of 1932 would see the creation of the dreaded Dust Bowl in our section of the Great Plains.

So, though my land lacked moisture, when seeding time came in September I drilled my wheat in dry ground. Two of my fields had enough subsoil moisture to bring the wheat up. The rest lay in a dry seedbed while I hoped for rain or snow to insure a start for it. Nothing happened.

In January a foot of snow fell, but that was all the moisture we had, and it was not enough to make a crop. Some of my wheat came up, but it was thin, sickly-looking stuff, with only two or three leaves to a plant. I drove to the irrigated district fifteen miles northwest of Garden City and by paying almost double the price quoted on the open market, I obtained some seed barley, which I proceeded to drill into the land where I had no hope of a wheat crop. This meant extra labor and expense, but I was bound to get from my land what it could be made to yield. New varieties of disaster awaited my every effort.

Most of my remaining wheat fell an easy prey to the first gales of February, and none of the wheat that was up in the region could long withstand the succeeding gales, which first chopped off the plants even with the ground, then proceeded to take the roots out. They did not stop there. They blew away the rich topsoil, leaving the subsoil exposed; and then kept sweeping away at the "hardpan," which is almost as hard as concrete.

This was something new and different from anything I had ever experienced before—a destroying force beyond my wildest imaginings. When some of my own fields started blowing, I was utterly bewildered.

I took counsel with some of my neighbors who had had greater experience, but received little in the way of encouragement. According to their information, there was little hope of saving a crop once the land had started blowing; and the only known method of checking the movement of the soil was the practice of strip listing. This meant running deep parallel furrows twenty or thirty feet apart, in an east and west direction, across the path of the prevailing winds. This tends to check the force of the wind along the ground, and allows the fine siltlike dust to fall into the open furrows.

Everyone in the region grasped at this slim chance to save a crop.

There was no frost in the ground, so I started strip listing right away, and found it a cold and disagreeable job. The thermometer would be just above freezing during the day, and would slip down below that point at night. It meant draining the tractor's radiator every night and refilling it every morning. It also meant that the pressure grease would be so stiff it was almost impossible to force it through the Zerk grease gun into the bearings of the tractor and the lister. The lubricating oil in the crankcase would be so congealed that it was

no easy job to start the motor. Morning after
morning I would crank until I was out of breath,
my tongue "dragging on the ground." Then I
would lean on the tractor until I recovered my
wind, and try again. Somehow, I always managed
to get the engine roaring at last.

In spite of every difficulty I stayed with the job
until all my land was listed; but more gales came
to render my efforts useless. With these gales all
traces of wheat and even barley vanished, but I
could not give up the struggle to save my land. I
well knew that only the top five inches of soil had
the fertility to produce good crops. If that soil
went, it would take ten years to work the land
back to its former state of productiveness. That
was what men said who had known similar conditions in the region twenty-five years before; so I
proceeded to list my land solid to check the soil
from blowing, determined to save that much from
the destructive forces of nature.

After the first shock of disappointment and be-
wilderment, the buoyant optimism of youth continued to sustain me. My wheat was gone, and
so was my barley, but I was not discouraged.
Once again I prepared and planted a considerable
acreage to maize.

We had twelve inches of rain in June, so, with
my maize all in, I had the assurance it would get
a good start; but the same rain meant tragedy in
the case of a neighbor of mine. The rain came

down so fast that the water had no chance to soak into the soil. It formed a lake in a wheat field a couple of miles west of me, and a number of men floated a raft on it. The raft overturned, and since none of the men knew how to swim, each thought only of self-preservation. Within twenty-five feet of the spot where their craft upset the water was only five feet deep, and all but one reached the shallow water and waded ashore. My neighbor became excited and was drowned in eight feet of water. Soon the water evaporated, or sank into the soil, but the ill-fated raft now lies half buried in the shifting blow dirt.

My maize attained a height of two feet, and my hopes continued to rise with the growing stalks; but you can never rely upon anything in the Great Plains. We get water enough in the course of the year to grow almost any kind of farm crop, but, for the most part, it comes all at once, with never a drop when you need it most. That was the way with my maize. Just when it was ready to head out, it began to suffer from lack of moisture. Several times each day I anxiously scanned the sky. Time after time clouds formed and united together, and my hopes would rise; but no rain came, and my hopes would fade and die. I lived in suspense, looking, hoping, wishing—expecting rain that did not come.

At last I acknowledged to myself that the maize was beyond hope of salvage; and never was there a wearier plowman than I, when I set myself to the task of seeding my fields to wheat once more, hoping to harvest a crop in 1933.

I had planted wheat in 1929, in 1930, and in 1931. I had planted barley and I had planted maize. I had planted five crops and harvested only one, for which I had received a miserably low price. You might have thought I would have become convinced that there was no profit in farming wheat in the Great Plains. But I was a glutton for punishment, and here I was planting wheat again, and still hoping.

Timely rains in October would have brought my wheat up before winter set in; but no moisture fell. Throughout the fall and winter we had neither rain nor snow, and when the usual gales came in February they were worse in velocity and endurance than any I had previously experienced.

With the gales came the dust. Sometimes it was so thick that it completely hid the sun. Visibility ranged from nothing to fifty feet, the former when the eyes were filled with dirt which could not be avoided, even with goggles. When dust is so fine that it will even penetrate to the works of fine watches and stop them, there is no way of controlling it. During a gale the dust would sift into the houses through crevices around the doors and windows, eventually to lie an inch or more deep all over the floors, and on tables, chairs, and beds.

Cleaning up a house after a dust storm is no

Maize field burnt up from lack of moisture.

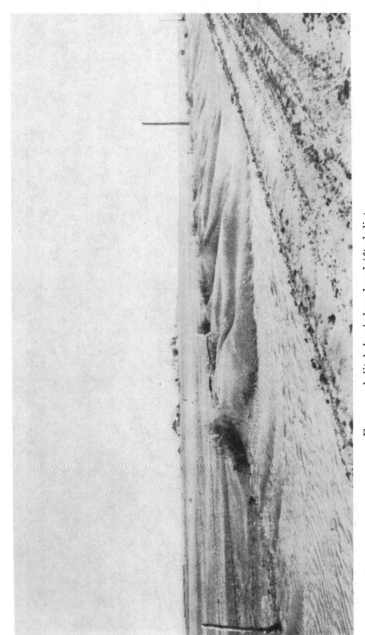

Fence and ditch buried under drifted dirt.

Two views of hedgerows buried by dirt.

This was once fine pasture land.

picnic. Disturb the dust and it flies up. Choked and gagging, the cleaner has to run outside to breathe. I speak from personal experience. Often I have used a scoop shovel to remove the great quantities from my house.

It was in 1933 that I saw, for the first time, loose thistles banked solidly behind the fences to the height of the top wire. The thistles retarded the blowing dirt, but only for a little while. In a day of blowing the trapped dust would cover both thistles and fences until only the post tops remained visible, then sweep on and on. There the fence would remain buried, because the time, effort, and money necessary to salvage it would represent more than the cost of a new fence to replace the old one.

Perhaps the Great Plains would sustain indefinitely a large population of stock farmers relying upon cattle and horses for their livelihood. But the insistent demand for wheat during the World War, both for home consumption and for the sustenance of the allies of the United States, started more and more farmers to break the sod and plant their land to wheat. "Wheat will win the war!" became a popular slogan, and the farmers planted and harvested wheat which was sold by the shipload to feed the British, the French, and the Belgians.

After the war was over, the growing of wheat continued to expand in the Great Plains. Eventually over two hundred million acres of it were planted, and not only plowing but harvesting, too, became a night and day job. The bosom of the land was being laid bare to the rains, the winds, and the sun; but don't blame the farmer alone. The General Land Office continued to encourage settlement, and there were glib salesmen in the field selling tractors, the most modern implements for plowing and cultivation, and combines to harvest the grain. Speculators from other lines of business took up wheat land or bought equipment and encouraged others to plant on shares. The farmers went into debt for land and machinery. Land appraised at about ten dollars an acre for grazing commanded a hundred dollars when planted in wheat, so there were mortgage interest and rising taxes to meet; but one good wheat crop sold at a good price might well yield returns equal to the profits to be earned in ten years of stock raising, and who was wise enough to be able to see into the future?

Land new to cultivation needed no fertilizing, so there was no reason to save the straw after the wheat was harvested. In most localities it was a common practice to burn off the straw with the stubble every second year, which left the ground easier to farm, and, incidentally, left it unprotected against the forces of erosion. I know of one field from which the straw was burned for four years in succession, and it outyielded adjacent fields farmed, except for the yearly burn-off, by the same methods.

Each farmer was doing what he thought best in the interest of the advancement of his own fortunes; but too-frequent plowings pulverized the soil to dust so fine it resembled ashes, and when moisture failed, such soil offered no resistance at all to the high winds of the plains.

There can be no doubt that breaking the sod to the plow over immense areas exposed the soil to the winds and hastened the destruction of thousands of square miles of land in the Great Plains; but overgrazing, too, was disastrous as proved by the Government estimates that the capacity of the range to support cattle has been reduced by 50 per cent. If overgrazing were the only fault, however, a great deal might now be accomplished towards restoring the wasted areas. Larger acreages under the control of individual stockmen, and co-operation with state and federal governments in the development of water supplies and the management of the range are plans that are being put in operation and are likely to be beneficial. The lands that have been swept clean of their topsoil or buried in dirt by the resulting dust storms offer a more difficult problem.

These dust storms offered a story that was new, unusual, and different from the general run of news, so, during the first two blow seasons, the newspapers played them up for all they were worth.

Headlines would read something like this: "Terrific Dust Storm Sweeps Western Kansas." The account that followed would be full and gripping, describing the all-enveloping darkness, halted traffic, ruined crops, livestock dying from eating dirt-filled food or from suffocation. After a while it all became an old story, except to the sufferers, and it came to be considered poor business to advertise the catastrophes.

Already people were vacating their homes and their lands; some because the dust was undermining their health, others because they were ruined financially and were forced to move to industrial centers where they hoped to get employment that would enable them to support their families and themselves.

Through the winter months most of the farmers had been working on relief, many of them men who had previously hired all their farm work done and had done no manual work themselves for years. The relief money they earned was not enough to provide the bare necessities of life for their families. Previously they had been comfortably off, or even well-to-do. Now they were just existing.

A salesman of my acquaintance, representing a well-known chain-wagon drug concern, told me of the many farm families unable to purchase supplies of which they were in desperate need. He was a soft-hearted fellow, and because he could not stand to see people suffering from privation

One of the thousands of farms abandoned to the scourge of dust and wind.

Wind tore off the top and caved in the sides of this steel bin.

Many houses were moved along the highways to be set up outside of the dust region.

Homes that cost several thousand dollars are now worth only what the lumber in them will bring.

MARICLE MERC. CO. — GROCERY DEPT. —

Two of the hundreds of business establishments that have been forced to close their doors.

The sign says "Business is good," but the farmer, with his family and his simple possessions, is heading east out of the dust area.

and was unable to offer help from his own slender resources, he applied for a transfer and was assigned to another territory.

There were only five of us in Meade County who listed our land. After a couple of hard blows every trace of my crop had vanished, but if the soil itself was not to disappear also, I had to check the land to keep it from blowing.

In common with the other four who followed this course, I had to face the additional handicap represented by negligent neighbors. Many of the farmers, after making a futile effort to save their crops, had no money for fuel and oil. The remaining few who still had funds that might have been applied to the work, simply did not feel like making the effort to check their land from blowing. They felt that losing a crop was tough enough, without battling the wind; so now the only time the land lay quiet was when the winds ceased to blow. The gales ceased in May.

There was a revival of optimism in the spring of 1933 when the Federal Government offered both spring and wheat crop loans, the former to help the farmers to grow maize for feed, the latter to encourage summer fallowing. The limit for both loans was five hundred dollars to an individual.

Summer fallowing is the practice of tilling the soil from May until wheat-seeding time, killing all weeds as soon as they start and thereby conserving all moisture that may fall during the spring and summer months. Wheat seeded in land worked by this method will survive drouths that destroy crops on land seeded every year, so the farmer was being helped to help himself.

Of course, there was considerable red tape connected with these loans. The applicant had to give a first mortgage on his crop, and if he did not own the land he farmed, he had to persuade his landlord to sign a waiver foregoing all claim to his share of the growing crop until the loan was repaid. All papers had to be sent to St. Louis for approval, and the procedure generally consumed a month's time.

The experience of planting crop after crop without return was becoming discouraging even to me, but I realized that to quit now would leave me a heavy loser in time, work, and money, so I became once more as optimistic as the others, with the sustaining knowledge that if I could raise one good crop and get a fair price for it, I would regain all that I had previously lost.

There was to be no 1933 wheat harvest for me, so I again prepared the soil and put in a big maize crop. After seeding, I cultivated twice; and then I saw another crop burn up for lack of moisture. That meant six crops lost to one harvested in four years of farming.

CHAPTER III

ENTER THE AAA

$\mathcal{S}OMETHING$ new and unexpected now came into existence to promise relief to the wheat farmers, to be hailed as a godsend by many and criticized by others as just another New Deal brainstorm. Of course I refer to the Agricultural Adjustment Administration which soon became known as the Triple A, or the AAA.

There were mouthy individuals who seized every opportunity to run down this entire program, talking as long as anyone would listen to them, condemning it as useless, crooked, revolutionary, or dictatorial; but it was noteworthy that when the first AAA payments were made available, shortly before Christmas, these same wordy critics made a beeline to the courthouse. They jostled and fell over each other in their mad scramble to be first in line to receive the allotment money, perhaps fearful that it would not hold out long enough to satisfy all applicants, though, naturally, applications had been filed and approved long before the money was made available.

Under the AAA agreement, a farmer had to keep out of cultivation 15 per cent of his total average acreage, using as the basis for his calculations the average number of acres he had had in crops during the three preceding seasons. In each county, the county average yield per acre was used as the basis of payment on the acreage held out of crop. Meade County's average was set at twelve and a half bushels to the acre, so that if a field had been in wheat continuously for the three previous years, the payment would be close to $185 on the entire field, or $10.50 an acre on the average acreage left out of crop.

Three acres came out of every quarter section for roads, but this left still too many acres for the money available, so an additional 2 per cent was deducted. The net result of the official calculations was that 129 acres could be put in crop from a quarter section that had been continuously farmed for three years.

On the other hand, if a field had been summer fallowed in any of the three previous years, this practice, praised as beneficial and formerly advocated, had the effect of cutting down considerably both on the payment that might be received and on the acreage that might now be put in crop under the terms of the AAA.

Each farmer had to draw maps of all the land under his control, showing roads, pasture, waste land, and even where the improvements he lived in were situated.

As was to be expected under the conditions existing in the wheat belt, human nature often revealed itself in greed and cupidity. There were farmers who reported their three years' average acreage in crop at a higher figure than was correct. One man included sixty acres that had never been broken until the spring of 1932. Another took an even longer chance. He entered sod as farming land, and broke it to the plow only after drawing his maps and reporting his acreage.

These are just two cases that happened to come under my own observation, and, of course, there were numerous others of a similar nature uncovered when the figures reported by individual farmers were published in the county weekly newspaper, accompanied by a notice inviting neighbors to report farmers who had padded their returns. This provided a unique opportunity to the spiteful, the revengeful, the envious, and the righteous, and most of the culprits were exposed in their trickery, and were compelled to correct their figures.

There were others, not at all culpable, who made honest mistakes in attempting to work out figures that were naturally confusing to those unaccustomed to such work; but they had to pay for their mistakes just the same.

Greed sometimes backfired on landowners who had never farmed their land themselves, or, at least, not for many years. They saw in the AAA plan an opportunity to enrich themselves at the expense of tenants. Under the ruling that first came out, the present farmer on the land was the one to receive the allotment payment, and many big landlords proceeded to oust tenants who had been farming their land for years. They took over the job of farming so as to qualify to collect the payments, which could only have served to frustrate the Government plan to assist the actual farmers. When reports of this practice reached Washington prompt action was taken. The rule was changed so as to make the farming tenant of the previous year the one eligible to receive the payment, even if he had been removed and was no longer farming the land. But even then there were landlords who sought to force their tenants to hand over to them more than their share of the money received from the Government.

One old gentleman who owns twenty-seven hundred acres of land northwest of my place had been renting his land under an agreement that gave him a quarter share of the crop as rental. That would have entitled him to one fourth of the allotment money, but he refused to sign the AAA agreement unless his tenant would give him one half.

Since both of these men were stubborn, neither would yield, and, consequently, no allotment money was obtained. The tenant moved off the land, very little of which has since been farmed. A mortgage company has a lien on the land for considerably more than its present worth, and probably only the recent passing of laws designed to protect distressed owners prevent immediate foreclosure.

The landowner, now older than the Biblical three-score years and ten, was reduced to working "on relief."

There were many farmers who failed to see that there could be any real overproduction, in spite of the big increase in the acreage planted to wheat over a period of years. Even the ruinously low prices obtained for the bumper crop of 1931 were ignored—largely because of President Roosevelt's oft-repeated statement that one third of the nation's population is classed as "underprivileged," and unable to purchase the necessities of life. The farmer is not responsible for faults in distribution or the national economic system, and he thought these might be remedied, so that the wheat he raised might find its way to those who needed it. As a matter of fact, many of the farmers were now themselves ill-nourished, ill-clothed, and ill-housed. Those who had received the wheat crop loan had already agreed to reduce their crop acreage by 20 per cent, while they would have to reduce it only 17 percent if they signed up under the AAA. Thus, they were in the position of having everything to gain and nothing to lose by complying with the new Government program. At the very least, the allotment payments would make it possible for them to continue to live on their farms a while longer; and the Government had enacted provisions which prevented creditors from seizing the allotment money.

For one reason or another there were very few wheat farmers who failed to sign under the AAA program.

Payments were to be made to the farmers in two installments, two thirds of the allotted amount to be received in September and the balance in June of the following year, after all operating expenses of the program had been deducted, including the salaries of the men employed to measure land and check claims, clerks, secretaries, and others. Naturally, with all the red tape that seems to be inseparable from Government activities, the first payment was delayed for three months or more. If my memory serves me faithfully, the afternoon of December 22 was set for the distribution of money in Meade County, and farmers on hand to receive their checks on that day formed the biggest crowd that ever stampeded the courthouse.

While awaiting allotment checks, we had to seed our wheat if we expected a crop. On the sixth of September we had a two-inch rain, and I drilled my wheat as soon as the ground was dry enough to use the drill. My usual luck held, and I had lots of extra work to do. On some of my land a few weeds had sprung up, and these became infested with grasshoppers. These pests chewed off the first leaves of the wheat plants as soon as they came through the soil, which was of course fatal to the tender plants. When more rain came in October, I proceeded to redrill nearly three hundred acres of my land. Three days of strong winds, unusual at that season, destroyed many fields, and they had to be reseeded.

In the midst of our own misfortunes, we may sometimes see humor in the situation of another no more fortunate than ourselves. I have in mind a man living southwest of me near the town of Plains. I would call him a self-approving man, because, no matter what he did or when he did it, he was always satisfied that his was the perfect time and method.

As soon as he had drilled his own wheat, this farmer confidently informed others that it was now too late to seed wheat. Unfortunately for his reputation as an expert, his crop disappeared with the high winds. He had to go to the elevator in town to purchase seed for redrilling, and had to replant his entire section of land. Was he humbled? Not a bit of it. He now stated with all assurance that this was the perfect time of the month to seed the land to wheat. Happy man!

When the usual February gales came in 1934, wheat that had been seeded in September and had survived the grasshoppers and the fall winds now had enough top growth to cover the ground entirely. This anchored the soil, and the winds damaged neither it nor the plants. Unfortunately, the wheat that had been redrilled was a different case. The plants did not attain sufficient growth to cover the ground before the gales started, and this ground soon showed a tendency to start blowing. I fought to hold my late wheat and was to some extent successful, losing only one quarter section of crop. However, though I claim some credit, the most important factor in my success was the fact that February and March witnessed fewer gales than we had experienced in former seasons, and the high winds subsided by the seventeenth of the latter month, which was considerably earlier than usual.

With my usual determined optimism, I decided to attempt to raise a barley crop on the land where I had already lost my wheat. At Leoti, 130 miles to the northwest of me, some farmers had been lucky enough to raise a crop of this grain the year before, so I went there to procure seed. I had to pay only a small premium above the market price, and considered myself fortunate that my loss was no greater. If I could now harvest what remained of my wheat, and could also harvest a fair barley crop, my year's labor would be well paid for. All I needed was rain in time to bring my crops to maturity.

In one respect part of my land is unfortunately situated. Lying a mile and a half west of my home there is a ridge, or hogback, about four miles in length, rising to a height of three hundred feet. Rain clouds usually approach my land from the northwest, and the hogback all too frequently splits such clouds, to my definite loss. When the clouds split, the two parts follow different paths. They come together again within a few miles, but in the interval an area of territory some seven miles long and five miles in width has been missed by the diverging clouds. As a result of this phenomenon, the land within this area, which includes some of my own, is often denied life-giving moisture that adjacent land receives. Even general rains are frequently lighter in their precipitation over this strip than they are elsewhere in the immediate vicinity.

As a matter of record, none of the farmers anywhere in the region had had a fair crop since 1931, a year when the drier strip I have described had yielded almost as good a crop as any of the surrounding fields. Nevertheless, with my crops already beginning to burn up in April for lack of rain, I found it particularly disheartening to miss a rain which my fields so badly needed. It was evening when a huge bank of dark black rain clouds formed in the northwest, and my hopes were high as I watched them slowly approaching in the direction of my land. Where the rain was already falling all the wheat crop had been blown out, but, while my crops were badly burnt, they still had a chance to make a good yield if they got rain. As the storm approached I could actually see the falling water in a heavy downpour, with blinding flashes of lightning accompanied by a continuous roar of thunder. Soon I could hear the rain as it fell. I could feel its coolness, smell it—almost taste it; and momentarily I expected to see it drench my

land. Then I watched the heavy clouds split into
two parts which reunited within a few miles, but
in the interim had passed me by, leaving me with a
sickening, deadening sense of hopelessness.

Two more rains came up, but they followed the
same course as the first, leaving my land devoid
of the moisture which would have meant the difference between failure and success to my thirsty
crops. Neighboring farmers whose land received
the benefits of these rains were assured of a crop
that year.

I plowed up some of my wheat and seeded the
ground to maize, but the less said about that
futile attempt to assure some kind of harvest, the
better. The maize did not even come up.

Variety is the spice of misfortune to the wheat
farmer! I have in mind one of my neighbors who
was fortunate enough to raise a successful crop
that year. He was farming seventeen hundred
acres of land and had one thousand acres in wheat.
He was one of those who had found the unaccustomed task of exact figuring of percentages a confusing one. His crop was well along when he was
informed that he had overseeded by eighty acres.
This farmer had been honest in his intentions, so
he was embarrassed as well as amazed; but, now
that the mistake had been made, he wanted to go
ahead and harvest the excess eighty and turn the
wheat crop over to the county commissioners, to
be distributed to the needy.

You will be able to guess what happened, if you have had any experience of small men elevated to petty office. The local allotment committee was made up of men who found great satisfaction in administering their office, and they were the ruling power in such matters, from whose decision there was no appeal. They would not consider the farmer's sane and philanthropic suggestion for the disposal of his surplus wheat. He was ordered to destroy it.

When it came to plowing up the wheat, the farmer naturally destroyed the poorest part of his crop, but even this would have yielded an average of twelve bushels to the acre, which was bad enough. Then, after he began harvesting his crop, another mistake in the figures came to light, this one representing a further excess of seventeen acres, which he was compelled to leave unharvested. Eventually, the breezes scattered the ripe grain on the ground.

My own feeling was that such wilful destruction of wheat after it had been grown was outside the bounds of human decency. Right in our own county there were men, women, and children in want, to whom the wasted grain would have been needed food. It was a flaunting in the face of Providence.

Of course, the outcome of such mistakes in arithmetic was not always the same. A man hired to farm land for the owner learned that he had thirty-three acres too much wheat to meet the terms of his allotment contract. He promptly called upon the county agent who was a supervisor of the allotment board and asked if he might cut the thirty-three acres of grain and stack it for use as cattle feed. The county agent said he might do this and still be complying with the regulations. Two months after the wheat had been cut and stacked, a member of the allotment committee came to the farm and peremptorily ordered the farmer to burn the stacks.

Naturally, the man protested. He explained that he had consulted the county agent before undertaking the labor of cutting and stacking the surplus. Now that the work was done, he did not see that he could be expected to burn the fodder.

The committee member was not impressed. He said that he, and not the county agent, made the final decisions in such matters, and the stacked wheat would have to be burned. Then the farmer told him what he thought of him and his board. He told him, as men will, where he might go, adding, "Maybe the stacks will be burned after the fight!"

"What fight?" the surprised committee member wanted to know, and he was told with grim emphasis, "The fight that's due to happen between you and me when you try to burn these stacks. If you come out of that fight whole and I don't, it will be then, and only then, that you'll burn them."

The farmer was a young man, over six feet in height, and weighing two hundred pounds. While peacefully inclined, he had the reputation of being tough when roused. The committee member was a man of discretion, so he departed in haste, and nothing further was heard from him on that particular farm. The grain and straw were fed to the cattle, as intended; and in due course the allotment payments were received in full.

As late as 1936 another case of high-handed destructiveness came to my attention. In this instance a farmer had seeded a field to oats, to be cut before the grain formed, to serve as feed for livestock. He had just begun cutting when a spell of rainy weather set in, and the grain reached maturity before he could resume cutting. The crop promised a fine yield of fifty to sixty bushels to the acre, so he proceeded to cut it with a binder, and stacked it. He intended to release it to the allotment officials to be distributed to poor farmers badly in need of feed for their cattle, but when he approached the allotment committee with his proposal they went up in the air.

Since his name was on the farm program contract, they insisted that the farmer must take orders from them; and their order was that the oat stacks must be burned. In this case a foolish order was carried out, but much to the disappointment of a generous man who had done a lot of work in the hope of benefiting others less fortunate than himself.

In 1934, when harvesttime came, I had only

one field of wheat for all my labor, and its yield
was only about three bushels to the acre. I harvested only enough to seed my land in the fall, and felt
pretty badly discouraged. I harbored no envy towards those of my neighbors who had had a crop.
They needed every bit of their good fortune. But
there was a degree of bitterness in my thoughts,
because I knew that all that had made the difference between our fortunes that year was the rain
that had blessed their land while passing mine by.

CHAPTER IV

WINDS OF CHANCE

WHAT proved to be about the toughest year in all my experience was now ahead, for I was determined to save my land and my business at all cost. I started to plow all my land, including the acreage that had been left idle in accordance with my allotment agreement. If I had summer fallowed this land, a successful crop would have meant a better crop than I could now expect; but I realized that if I was going to have any crop at all, I would have to hold the land from blowing. With this in mind I had permitted my idle land to grow to weeds and thistles. After attaining a growth of a foot or so they all dried up in April. By now plowing in the trash of weeds and thistles I hoped that these would help prevent the soil from blowing the following spring.

Taking advantage of an inch of rain that fell on the first day of September, I started drilling, determined to get my wheat in as speedily as possible. I knew that the inch of moisture that had fallen was barely enough to insure my crop's coming up, and getting the seed in early meant giving the wheat its best chance to make sufficient growth to cover the ground before the coming of winter. Experience had demonstrated beyond question that, lacking this sufficient start, it would all vanish in the spring when the gales started to blow.

Of course, more moisture before planting might have meant faster and better growth; but that is the kind of gamble the farmer has to take. If more moisture came, it might be too late to do any good, for, no matter how much precipitation we may have after the cold and freezing weather has set in, it offers no help towards saving the crop from the blow winds ahead.

Perhaps I should explain that rain does not of itself stop the soil from blowing once the high winds have started and the land has begun to move. Of course it will check it as long as the surface is wet, but it can happen that we have a heavy rain one day and the next day the land will be blowing as badly as formerly. Rain is helpful in this respect only when it comes sufficiently in advance of the blowing season to insure sufficient growth of plant life to anchor the soil.

No rain at all came that fall after I had planted my wheat. Two of my fields died for lack of moisture, two others had about half a stand, and I had one remaining quarter section which I considered good, though, as a matter of fact, it had only a little top growth.

Along in the latter part of January we headed into weather that can only be described as "unusual" for our section. It was something I personally had never seen before nor had ever expected to happen at that season, a twenty-four-hour general rain which soaked into the dry soil as fast as it fell, accompanied by mild temperatures that prevailed from then on.

I had known of wheat to be seeded in the fall in dry soil, which, after lying in a dry seedbed, had come up with the coming of snow in February, and had produced a good crop. I had also seen a good crop yield from land seeded in February; and I still had some wheat in the bin. The odds were about one hundred to one against me, but I had taken chances before and was prepared to take another, which I did by redrilling one of the quarter sections on which my wheat had failed to survive.

After I had gambled my seed wheat, I awaited the outcome with both interest and hope. The middle of February came and went, and we had plenty of optimists among us who now made the bold prediction that the blowing years were past and we might now look forward to several years of favorable conditions and profitable crops. In the meantime my quarter section of February-planted wheat had come up and was looking fine, so I began to hope that the soothsayers might be right.

All optimistic prophets were confounded when the twenty-second day of February came and the gales started, and it seemed as if the spirits of the storm were intent upon making up for the delay. The winds unleashed their fury with a force beyond anything we had previously experienced; and one storm followed closely upon the heels of another until it seemed as if the whole surface of the earth would be blown away.

In my own case, I soon knew that I was going to have a battle on my hands. After three winds in four days, every bit of my land except one solitary quarter section was on the move, and I had no alternative but to go out once more and put forth every effort to save my crop by stopping the land from blowing.

Most of the farmers in our section use an adapted one-way in preference to a lister. By removing the disks from the shaft and putting back only four of them, equally spaced, we have an implement that does the work satisfactorily, with the advantage that land listed in this way is much more easily worked level again when the blow season is over and the rains commence.

In my effort to save my crop, I used my adapted one-way to throw up four furrows at a time and spaced the swaths fifteen feet apart. In this way I expected to provide a temporary check which would hold the land until the warmer weather came. Then the wheat would grow more rapidly until it got big enough to protect itself from the relentless winds.

My hope that I would yet harvest some wheat was bolstered by the fall of an inch of rain on the first day of March. That promised faster growth if only I could continue to prevent further blowing of my land.

I soon learned that this was going to be no easy matter to accomplish, for the gales again started with renewed vigor. Indeed, they were more destructive than ever, wreaking their vengeance even on the best wheat I had; namely, the one field that had not previously started to blow.

This called for heroic measures, because there was so much blow dirt on the field, caught from adjacent land in past blow seasons, that I knew strip ridging would be ineffectual to stop it even against one wind. Though the tops of the plants had been burned by the electricity in the air caused by the moving dirt, the wheat in this field was still alive. I knew that if I expected to hold it, I would have to ridge up the land solid. Not only had I my own wheat to consider, but, also, the field belonging to a neighbor that lay just north of my shifting field. If I did not check my land, the dirt from it would ruin my neighbor's wheat in short order, and that was against my principles. In both the two preceding years, this man's land had blown on to mine, and he had made no effort at all to check it, but I had never so far been responsible for the loss of another man's crop, and I was not yet ready to adopt the attitude of carelessness towards the welfare of others that was becoming all too prevalent.

Since my neighbor's land lay to the north, I started working along the north side and, in a couple of days, had completed ridging half the area of my field when I caught a heavy cold. The cold settled on my lungs and confined me to the house for a week, and if that kind of cold causes discomfort anywhere, it is just a little worse in the Dust Bowl when the high winds are blowing and the fine dirt particles are settling everywhere in the house, irritating the delicate membranes of the nose and throat, and of the lungs too. While I remained indoors, we experienced three gales from the northwest, and they started the south part of my field to blow. Here, on the south, my land was bounded by a road, but that was no effective barrier against blow dirt. Beyond the road lay another man's land, a field which had been lying idle for allotment benefits, and it was overgrown with thistles to the height of a foot or more. They formed an effective trap for the blow dirt that was now coming from my land. It really was not my dirt at all, since I had only borrowed it, so to speak, during previous storms, but now it formed a dirt bank a hundred feet wide, half a mile long, and two feet high—on my neighbor's field.

Now this farmer's land, totally abandoned to the whims of the wind, had helped ruin my crops for three years in succession, and he had never once checked it for my benefit. Back in 1933, his topsoil had shifted over my land every time the wind blew from the southward, and he had made no attempt to stop it. He did list the field in July, but by that time the blow season was long past. In May, while I was plowing my land, then drilling to maize, there had been days when I could not keep my eyes open, because of the dust blowing from his land. But he had continued to let it blow and blow until a large part of my maize crop went with it. When my wheat had blown out in 1934, I had drilled this same field to barley which the drouth of that year cut short. In May that year this man had come to me to ask for help. He had cattle, and no feed for them; and he wanted to pasture the animals in my field. I had always been willing to lend a helping hand to others when conditions made it possible, so I had readily consented to his proposal.

Now, for once, it was my land that was blowing on his, and you may be sure he wanted something done about it right away. I do not suppose he had nerve enough to come over to offer his protest in person; and he did not have to. He had a son-in-law living on the place, and to that extent dependent on him, so he elected him to be his ambassador.

The son-in-law was a tall, lanky man whose slow-drawling speech stamped him as a Southerner, and his expression was sheepish when he delivered the older man's message; to-wit, that he wanted me to check my land from blowing.

I was still under par as the result of my spell of illness, but I verily believe if the farmer had come himself on that errand, I would have done my best to send him to the hospital, so I suppose it was just as well he had chosen to send a go-between. I stood looking at the man, inwardly boiling as I recalled the years just past, and so I stood until my anger began to cool. Then I promised that I would start listing my blowing field next day, and he went off to report to his father-in-law.

I leave this case without comment beyond stating that I carried out my promise. There are many people like my neighbor, careless about the welfare of others but much concerned about their own. I have met others of similar disposition and have never discovered the effective counterattack. I had to hold my land for my own sake as well as his, so I went about the job with what cheerfulness I could muster.

By the time I had gone over that field, three others were moving. The furrows soon filled level with blow dirt, and the winds continued worse than ever. Already my wheat in these fields was dead, but I continued to work, ridging them up solid to check their movement. I had become a slave to the land under the merciless lash of the winds, and I began to wonder if I would ever again breathe clean air.

Now it was April, and out of all the land I had planted to wheat I had left only one quarter section with crop, one of those on which I had obtained half a stand.

However, I was not alone in my plight—far from it. As a matter of fact, only a few scattering

A listed field already beginning to fill up with blowing dirt.

The tenacious roots of the soapweed hold when all else blows away; their elevation shows that three feet of the original soil has gone off in clouds of dust.

Here lies expensive machinery.

A ten-foot plow buried under blow dirt. In the background, an abandoned home.

A house buried by dirt.

Wheels that no longer turn.

fields in the region still had a crop, so we were all in the same boat. My one field was in better shape than any other, according to the opinion voiced by neighbors. Even to me, it looked as if I might harvest between two and three thousand bushels of wheat, which would mean something to show for my year's work. How much of it I actually harvested I shall leave to another chapter to reveal.

CHAPTER V

A MAIZE KING ABDICATES

PREACHERS, in all sincerity, persistently teach the blessings of adversity, and I suppose it is true that the habit of facing difficulties with courage develops character and resourcefulness. My experience in the Dust Bowl, however, has taught me that there is another side to the picture, and I now believe that too much adversity, or adversity too long continued, breaks down morale.

One of my neighbors has also been one of my closest friends ever since I was a boy. He is a bachelor like myself, and is now around fifty. He owned his place free from mortgage, and his machinery was all paid for. He had been fortunate enough to raise a maize crop of six thousand bushels in 1933, when all other crops in the neighbodhood had failed. His possessions represented the fruits of his productive years; but now he had become disgusted and discouraged and was ready to leave Meade County forever; and he wanted me to go with him.

Surprised to learn that my friend was ready to admit defeat, I set myself the task of trying to convince him that the course he proposed would be a mistake. I argued that it would be foolish for him to walk out, since he was by no means compelled to such a course. Certainly he could not dispose of his holdings at a time when, as the result of the drouth, no one could be found to buy them, at any price; but it had taken the best years of his life to acquire his property, and it was still valuable, and all he had. He knew nothing but farming, and for a man of his age with no special trade it would be practically impossible to get employment anywhere at any sort of wages that would mean a living.

He listened patiently, but was far from being convinced by my arguments, so, having finished working my own land for the time being, I said that I would pull out with my outfit and we would work over his four quarter sections with one-way ridging, together.

This offer to help cheered him considerably, and we started on the job, but after two days I had difficulty keeping him at it. The will to strive was no longer behind his efforts. Almost every day thereafter he suggested that we give up and go to town in search of diversion. When I bluntly refused to consider this course, he would still hang back, offering the slim excuse that he was not feeling up to par.

"You don't need to work if you don't feel like it," I would tell him. "You stay at home. I'll go out and finish the job."

He was not that sort of man, so he naturally

refused to let me work his land alone. After our morning discussion he would always start his tractor and follow mine to the field. What he wanted to do was let the land go. He no longer had any interest for the work we were doing, and when the dust was blowing, I believe he even hated me for my persistence. When he received his allotment payment in September, he wanted to pay me for the work I had done, and insisted that I should take the money he tendered; but my efforts had been a voluntary offering for friendship's sake, and I could not accept payment. I would have felt more than repaid if I could have seen this friend of mine snap back to his old courageous outlook, for I was impatient with his attitude. The time was not far distant when I too would experience the lethargy that comes over a man when sustaining hope and faith in the future are gone, but I had no suspicion of this at the time.

Soon after we had finished working over my friend's fields, we learned that the wind had still a few tricks to play that year. Nature had hitherto only been playing with us, and now unleashed a series of gales far more terrible than any we had previously experienced. One of these high winds blew continuously for a period of one hundred hours; but the gale which started at two o'clock on the fourteenth of April was much worse while it lasted. This was the blackest day within the memory of living man, and on that day the dramatically descriptive phrase, "The Black Blizzard," was coined, inspired by the rolling dust clouds that blotted out the sun.

Alfred M. Landon was Governor of Kansas at that time, and he made a trip through the western part of the state to see for himself the blowing conditions as they existed. He was astounded by what he saw; and it is a fact that no one can realize what a black blizzard is like until he has actually seen one with his own eyes and experienced its terrors. When he realized the unbearable handicaps under which the farmers of the Dust Bowl were struggling, including the destruction of crops by the blowing of the soil, the Governor lost no time in communicating with Washington. It was not long until the Federal Government made funds available to farmers who needed financial help to do the necessary work to check the blowing of their fields.

As usual, there was much red tape involved, and the conditions attached were humiliating to many farmers who had long taken pride in their independence. In order to obtain a share of the funds available for the work, the farmer had to make application to the county agent, and sign papers stating that he was a pauper, unable to borrow the necessary money to purchase fuel and oil to list his land. Only then would he be given a credit slip entitling him to the supplies he needed most.

It is not my intention to criticize the regulations

imposed, but only to raise a question for consideration by thoughtful people. The destruction of millions of acres in the Great Plains region by the blowing away of the topsoil is a national loss affecting not only the present generation, but also many generations to come. The blame for present conditions attaches not alone to farmers, either individually or collectively, but also to railroads, machinery manufacturers, and the Government itself. The Government is spending many millions of dollars, experimentally, in expensive efforts to reclaim selected portions of wasteland in the Great Plains region. It would seem that the least expensive way of checking the spread of the destruction now going on in the Great Plains would be to assist the farmer to stop his land from blowing, as an important measure of conservation, without pauperizing the farmer in the process. Either the money granted the farmer for this purpose is expended in the national interest, or it is an expenditure not justified at all.

Of course, there is another side to the question, involving the many flaws to be found in our common human nature. By far the greater part of the farmers in Meade County acknowledged themselves paupers and received their share of the fund offered. A lot of them needed assistance, but there were many others who simply took advantage of another opportunity to get Government money by the simple process of signing a false affidavit.

Among this latter group were some who owned their farms and had no indebtedness. One was a man who owned property in different sections of the state. Perhaps he needed the help, for he was a bullheaded, contrary man who frequently took heavy losses because of his stubbornness. In more prosperous days he raised several good crops which he piled on the ground rather than accept a price less than he demanded, and he made his demands regardless of the market. Later, after his grain had been badly damaged by the elements, he might sell it for half the amount he had previously been offered; or, if he wished, he would let the entire crop rot. Not so long ago he was hauling to market wheat that he had raised in 1929. It was stringy, light, worm-eaten stuff that brought thirty or forty cents a bushel, because it could only be used for the making of bran and shorts. While I do not know it, I would almost be willing to gamble that he still has some of this old wheat in his bins.

There were some among the applicants who had recently purchased new automobiles; and two of them had spent the winter enjoying life on the coast of Texas, in the lower Rio Grande Valley. Of course, one can see that these might well have been out of cash to buy gasoline and oil for their tractors.

So far I had never applied for a Government dole, and I was not yet ready to begin doing so; but then I had no new car, nor had I sojourned in the sunny southland for the winter, and that makes a difference. There were five other farmers in our locality who held to the same policy of independence, and I was glad to have their company.

With the winds continuing, it was not long before all the land I had ridged up solidly needed working again. Adjoining fields, farmed by others and never checked, began moving over on mine, and once the dirt had filled my furrows level, my own land began to blow more than ever. I had only one quarter section of wheat remaining, and half of that now went up in dust. I diligently worked over the other half in the hope that I might be successful in saving enough wheat to provide the necessary seed for another crop. That job completed, I began splitting ridges on my other fields, by which method I could cover up the blow dirt that choked the old furrows.

It was no pleasant task, for nearly every day now the winds were blowing up the dust. When the wind blew, I had to drive blind, often unable to see the radiator cap on my tractor. Long after other farmers had ceased trying, I was still determined to check my land, at any cost, so I kept going, driving by guess and instinct.

You can't live continuously in dust like that, day after day, without suffering some ill effects. I was so filled with dust that it affected both my hearing and sight. There were times when I listened in vain to hear the engine exhaust, which is normally loud enough to be classed as a roar; and objects, no matter how close they might be, would seem to rise like huge mountains, then dwindle to nothing before my eyes.

I am considered a good mechanic, and I usually keep my equipment in first-class condition, which is a sound practice that saves me many hours of time that might otherwise be lost. But one day I permitted my tractor to throw a connecting-rod bearing while I was driving it in the field, and I did not hear a thing. As a matter of fact, I did not suspect the damage until the following morning when I started the engine at sunup, while the wind was napping.

By the time I had finished splitting ridges, May had arrived, but the gales continued to sweep over the land. In previous years within our experience the high winds had run their course by the end of April, or soon after, but there was no letup as yet.

Nature seems to have been on a veritable rampage that year, for floods menaced various sections of the nation over a wide area which included western Nebraska and the northwest portion of Kansas. Madly swirling waters swept away everything in their course. Homes were wrecked, bridges and roads demolished, and thousands of livestock killed. Possessions that men had worked a lifetime to accumulate were wiped out in a twinkling. The appalling property loss mounted into the millions of dollars, and many of the

owners of the destroyed property considered themselves fortunate to have escaped with their lives.
As a matter of fact, the human victims caught in
the muddy torrents were numerous enough. At
least 147 persons met death by drowning in the
states of Kansas and Nebraska. Thirteen flood victims lay side by side at one time on Main Street in
St. Francis, Kansas.

In marked contrast with the flooded areas of the
state, our part of western Kansas remained in the
grip of the dust menace. Our lands lay parched
while the topsoil of many fine fields went skyward,
and these conditions prevailed until the twenty-
fifth of May. Then, at last, the rain came, with
a precipitation of five inches during the ensuing
two days and nights, which effectively put an end
to the blowing of the land for that season.

With the coming of rain the whole aspect of the
country changed, and I felt again the buoyancy of
young manhood. Actually, my hopes soared, for
I had worked faithfully to save the little wheat that
was still left to me, and I now felt confident that
I was going to have the satisfaction of harvesting
it.

As further encouragement, another rain fell on
the first of June, a small cloudburst that drenched
the land in the short space of half an hour and
accomplished some good, though most of the water
ran off into the lagoons.

As soon as the topsoil had dried after the first

rain, I commenced plowing my fields, leveling down the ridges. The weather was exceptionally good for the time of year, but it remained so chilly that one of my friends was wearing his sheepskin coat and claimed that he was not a bit too warm. There were days in the field when I wished I had brought my own sheepskin with me, and there were at least a couple of evenings when I had to start a fire in the heating stove in order to be comfortable.

I was working from daylight until dark, which enabled me to accomplish wonders those lengthening days. I plowed six hundred acres of my land, and planned to plant all of it to maize. Already, however, there was a lack of sufficient moisture in the soil, so I planted only part of it. I seeded more of my land to maize in June, and the rest of it in July, after an inch of rain had fallen that month. None of this discouraged me, because by having my crops strung out in the time of planting, I figured that I was increasing my chances. If rain came too late to help one field, it might be just in time to help another, so I was likely to harvest at least some of my maize whatever happened; and, with a couple of good rains at the right time, I had a good chance of a harvest from my whole six hundred acres planted to this crop. I had a larger acreage of land in this crop than any other farmer in the locality, so they called me the "Maize King," and it did not hurt my feelings a bit. I had fought hard to deserve success, and if I could not now expect any considerable wheat harvest, maize would serve very well as a substitute.

By the time I had completed the seeding of my last quarter section of maize, the first quarter I had planted was ready to cultivate. Though I had to go over it twice to get all the weeds out, I went at the task with as much enthusiasm as I had brought to the plowing and planting; and the roar of my tractor was music in my ears.

I did not have to cultivate my other fields, because no rain had come to bring the weeds up after planting, and while this relieved me of labor, it also meant a lowering in the barometer of my expectations, for if my fields did not get rain, neither could I expect a good crop.

By the middle of July the first maize I had planted was beginning to burn in a couple of places. When blow dirt is composed of the topsoil from adjacent fields, it is the very cream of productive soil, and there were blow drifts that I had seeded on this field. On these drifts the maize had grown more rapidly than anywhere else, despite the lack of sufficient moisture, and now, with moisture still lacking, it began to deteriorate more quickly than any of the rest.

On the other hand, I had already lost the precious wheat I had worked so diligently to save, but from an entirely different cause. On account of too much moisture coming at one time, the dreaded black rust had affected my wheat and destroyed it, so I proceeded to plow it up. On one quarter section of my land there was blow dirt lying to a depth of from one to two feet, all over the field, and this I decided not to touch with the plow. I was ashamed to let it go unplowed, because I did not believe that leaving it could be classed as farming the land in a workmanlike manner suitable for wheat; but, on the other hand, there had not been much growth of weeds over the blow dirt, and what had grown were drying up, and I knew that if I did plow the field, it would blow out in the spring. So I decided to do what I thought best in the circumstances, and I believed that if I drilled wheat in the ridges, that method would give me my best chance for a crop the following year.

There was one afternoon around the first of August when a rainstorm came up from the northwest, and I hoped for rain. Here was a time when I needed a break, and I watched the approaching storm in the belief that rain now would assure me a good crop from my earliest maize and be of considerable benefit to the rest. I have already told about the fatal ridge that so often splits the rain clouds approaching my land, and it split this one. Once split, the clouds followed their all-too-familiar course, and the storm came no nearer my land than most of those which come from the northwest.

But I was by no means ready to accept defeat, and I congratulated myself on the circumstances that had led me to space my plantings. Even if my first maize failed to produce a crop, I still had a chance for later rains to assure me a harvest from my other fields.

To illustrate the narrowness of the margin that separates the farmer from victory or defeat, I want to refer again to that early August rain. If it had been a general rain falling over a large territory, the fact that it missed my land would not necessarily have been fatal to my crop. It would have cooled off the atmosphere sufficiently to have modified the intensity of the hot winds which soon after began to blow over the land.

As it was, my first maize was beyond help by the first of September, and then my two remaining fields began to burn.

But the weather became cooler, cool enough that even a local rain might be counted on to revive vegetation. With such a rain, the later-planted portion of my maize might still make a crop, but it would have to have moisture soon—very soon. Desperately I clung to hope until the middle of the month; and then I acknowledged to myself that my maize crop was beyond saving. The long-awaited, desperately needed rain did not come until the twenty-seventh of September, and it was too late to be of any use to me.

When I knew that my crop was irrevocably gone I experienced a deathly feeling which, I hope, can affect a man only once in a lifetime. My dreams and ambitions had been flouted by nature, and my shattered ideals seemed gone forever. The very desire to make a success of my life was gone; the spirit and urge to strive were dead within me. Fate had dealt me a cruel blow above which I felt utterly unable to rise. Season after season I had planted two, and sometimes three, crops. I had worked incessantly to gain a harvest, or to keep my land from blowing, and no effort of mine had proved fruitful. Words are useless to describe the sensation a human being experiences when the thin thread of faith snaps. I had reached the depths of utter despair.

The scars of that year are with me still. I can never again be the determined optimist I once was; but the world did not come to an end, and, before the first of September I had taken advantage of a slight dip in the market to buy seed wheat at $1.04 a bushel. With the arrival of allotment checks all the farmers around me were buying seed wheat. By the first of October I was out in the fields again —drilling wheat.

CHAPTER VI

BLACK BLIZZARD

DUST storms had become a familiar story in the Great Plains, but 1935 was the first year that dust from this area floated in huge black cloud formations so far east as to pass over Washington, D. C.

The sight caused not a little consternation. Senators, representatives, and Government officials stared wide-eyed in astonishment, and had no idea of the origin of the massed clouds of black dust sailing through space above them. Then a congressman from Kansas who had many times seen the same thing in his home state, explained the phenomenon to his colleagues, and Washington began to realize what the Great Plains farmers had been complaining about.

These same low, heavy, dirt-laden clouds have often been sighted far out at sea, in the Atlantic, the Pacific, and in the Gulf of Mexico; all of which gives point to the case of the farmer who was seen staring intently towards the sky, in one of our western towns, during a strong northwester.

"What's the attraction?" an inquisitive friend asked. The terse reply was, "I just saw a quarter section of my wheat passing over town."

Oncoming dust storm at its worst.

A day of the "black blizzard."

Darkness and dust settle upon the land.

This was a highway.

The black object at right is the top of an automobile. The rest is
buried under the dirt.

Only those who have been caught out in a "black blizzard" can have more than a faint conception of its terrors. When the soil has become finely pulverized by too much working over, by the action of water followed by wind, or, particularly, when the surface is blow dirt from a previous storm, the dust begins to blow with only a slight breeze. As it continues to rise into the air it becomes thicker and thicker, obscuring the landscape and continuing to grow in density until vision is reduced to a thousand yards, or less. If this is to be a real dust storm, a typical black blizzard of the Dust Bowl, the wind increases its velocity until it is blowing at forty to fifty miles an hour. Soon everything is moving—the land is blowing, both farm land and pasture alike. The fine dirt is sweeping along at express-train speed, and when the very sun is blotted out, visibility is reduced to some fifty feet; or perhaps you cannot see at all, because the dust has blinded you, and even goggles are useless to prevent the fine particles from sifting into your eyes, though they break the force of the driving dirt.

Thus it is when the observer is within the area of a storm's inception. At other times a cloud is seen to be approaching from a distance of many miles. Already it has the banked appearance of a cumulus cloud, but it is black instead of white, and it hangs low, seeming to hug the earth. Instead of being slow to change its form, it appears to be rolling on itself from the crest downward. As it sweeps onward, the landscape is progressively blotted out. Birds fly in terror before the storm, and only those that are strong of wing may escape. The smaller birds fly until they are exhausted, then fall to the ground, to share the fate of the thousands of jack rabbits which perish from suffocation.

Human beings run for their lives, if there is any safe place within reach. Some run anyway, well knowing that unless shelter is reached, they may be victims of the same fate that overtakes the birds and the jack rabbits. Many harrowing tales of the Dust Bowl have been told by hitchhikers caught out in one of these storms, with no certain knowledge of the region to guide them to a place of safety.

There are many car owners who make it a policy never to pick up a hitchhiker, for the reason that good-natured drivers have sometimes been victimized. There have been cases of robbery—even murder. I know of one insurance man who has adopted the resolution never to pick up a stranger on the road, because of an experience in a dust storm.

He was driving from Pueblo, Colorado, to attend a conference at Kansas City, Missouri, and readily consented to give a lift to a young couple encountered on the road. All went well until after dark, somewhere in the vicinity of Ulysses, Kansas, when they headed into a black blizzard.

Between the darkness, and the driving dust,

conditions made further progress impossible. It was the first time either of the young people had experienced one of these storms, and they became frightened. They wanted to leave the car and try to reach the shelter of some farmhouse.

The insurance man got the young husband out of the car, on the pretext of examining the tires, and persuaded him that their best chance, and practically their only chance to survive the storm was to stay with the car; and, together, they set themselves to persuade the young woman to accept the older man's judgment.

As they gasped for air in the choking dust, which could by no means be kept out of the car, the woman became hysterical, and they had to use force to hold her in the car. She bit and clawed in her frenzy of fear and rage, but they held her helpless, knowing that if she once got away from them into the storm, she would soon drop from exhaustion and, in all probability, die from suffocation.

All through the long night they had to hold her; but the storm broke about daylight, and the car owner took his guests on to Kansas City. He is set against picking up wayfarers now, not so much because of the unpleasantness of this experience, so far as he was concerned, but because he feels that if these two young people had left the car and died, he would have been in a measure responsible for their deaths.

Automobile travel is always extremely hazardous during a severe dust storm. Unable to see more than a few yards ahead, motorists will nevertheless continue to drive on, in the desperate hope of reaching some refuge more substantial than the car itself. Of course, they may succeed in reaching a farmhouse, if only one that has been abandoned by the owners or tenants, but even lighted windows are often invisible beyond a short distance. There is always the possibility of driving off a road no longer defined, where ditches are filled level with drifting dirt. Head-on collisions are frequent, often attended with injury to the occupants of the cars involved, and sometimes with death.

Cars often stall on the road during a dust storm, from no cause other than that the air is surcharged with electricity due to the friction of the dust particles. The ignition system fails to function, and while the conditions causing the failure continue, it is usually quite impossible to start the car. All too often the driver has no idea why his car has stopped, and he will continue to work until he becomes exhausted by his futile efforts to start the motor. Finally, he will set out in a desperate search for shelter. Many have died in such circumstances; and the tragic irony of it is that a car stalled from this cause will start right away, with no trouble at all, as soon as the storm has subsided.

Generally speaking, the wisest course for the motorist caught in a bad dust storm is to stay with his car, unless there is a more substantial shelter actually in sight. Once he has left it, he will probably be unable to find a house, and he may be likewise unable to locate his car again.

I had one experience in a dust storm that might have been a great deal worse if the storm had lasted longer than it did. It was during a pretty fierce gale with dust filling the sky, though none of the fields near my place were blowing, that a friend came over to ask me to accompany him on an errand that would take us out only about thirty miles. Since the land was not blowing in our immediate vicinity, I consented to go, and, at my friend's request, I took the wheel of the car, to drive. We followed a little-used road for a while, before turning into a well-traveled highway, and soon found ourselves in the blowing area. The farther we progressed, the worst the dust became. Soon there was no visibility left worth mentioning. Even the headlights were of no help in driving, because their reflection from the dust particles was thrown back directly into my eyes.

Fully alive to our danger, I kept on the alert for a crossroad running eastward, in which direction lay home and safety, but in this I had no luck, so I felt impelled to resort to the dangerous expedient of making a U turn on the highway. I was driving blind, and if another car happened to be coming along, its driver would be as blind as I, so I was taking the chance of a collision.

With the car across the road, I had to shift gears,

letting the motor idle for this purpose. The motor stalled, owing to static. As long as the motor had been turning rapidly, the ignition system had not been affected, at least not to the point of stalling; but now that the motor was dead, I knew there was only a slim chance that I might succeed in getting it started again. With the position of the car across the highway, I had a lively fear that we would be struck by some other motorist as foolish as we had been in getting caught out in that inferno of dust, but I kept calm as I tried persistently to coax my engine back to life. In a few minutes my patience and self-control were rewarded. The motor took hold, and with a sense of tremendous relief, I very cautiously started the car in the direction opposite to that in which we had previously been traveling.

At crawling pace, I edged the car back over the road for half a mile or so until I saw a farmhouse dimly discernible from the highway. I drove into the yard and found a man there who was trying to start his car. I was frank enough to admit I was lost, so it was a relief to encounter a human being who might be expected to know where we were. I lowered the window to ask, and, with a wrench in one hand and a pair of pliers in the other, the man straightened up, wiped the dirt from his eyes, and shook his head.

"Buddy," he said, "you are a long ways from nowhere."

"I know that," I responded with a grin. "But where are we from Sublette or Copeland?"

"Nine miles southeast of Sublette," he told me.

This information enabled me to orient myself, which meant a load off my mind, and I was now curious to know why he was working on his car during a dust storm, right there in his own yard. Then I learned that the farmhouse was deserted, and that he was the operator of a road maintainer which was parked within a stone's throw of us. He had started work that morning and had scraped two feet of blow dirt from the highway in one place. The storm had forced him to quit, and there was nothing to show that he had done anything, since the dirt had drifted over the highway as badly as before. For a couple of hours he had been trying to get his car started, and had discovered that the switch was filled up with dirt and would not make connection.

At first I was inclined to believe his trouble was the same that I had experienced, that is, the electricity in the air, affecting the ignition system; but when I examined the switch, I soon saw that he had diagnosed the trouble correctly. There was a short circuit in that switch, and, until that was cured, he was stuck. Learning that he lived at Sublette, I offered to drive him home, with the suggestion that it would be an easier and more pleasant task to fix the switch after the wind had died down and the dust had settled. However, he said if he did not get the car running, and if the wind did not calm down, he was going to spend the night at the deserted farmhouse, so we left him with our good wishes, and accepted his, and started on our way.

When we reached home, the gale was already slackening, and everything was calm by ten o'clock, though there was still plenty of dust in the air. By midnight this dust lay half an inch thick over everything in the house; and then, at two o'clock in the morning, one of the worst gales we had ever known swept out of the northwest. It kept blowing for twenty hours, and both my friend and I had reason to congratulate ourselves that we had met the man from Sublette and through the directions he had given us had succeeded in reaching home when we did. I shall have occasion to mention this storm again in another chapter.

Cars, trucks, and tractors are all subject to internal dust which sifts into the bearings and clogs the working parts. I have seen automobile motors that have been ruined from a single day's operation during a dust storm, because the air cleaner was not performing its function; but even when precautions have been taken to see that all equipment is working efficiently, the dust will find its way into the motor. The usual symptom is overheating, and frequent overhauling is necessary to keep the engine operating in a fairly satisfactory manner during the blowing season. When the air cleaner fails, however, complete ruin to the motor is a matter of only a short time, because the dust eats away valves, rings, and pistons, and causes grooves in the cylinder walls too deep to be remedied by the usual expedient of reboring. Nor is this the limit of the damage done. Dust works down into the crankcase, where it speedily ruins the camshaft and the connecting rods, and flattens even the crankshaft, so that it becomes useless.

As might be expected, there is no compensation to be expected from the manufacturer, and claims for replacement fall upon deaf ears. The owner of the machine is told that if he had taken just a little time out to test the operation of his air cleaner, the damage would not have occurred, and, in all fairness, it will have to be admitted that this is usually true.

One day in Meade I saw an expensive automobile, with only a thousand miles of travel registered on the speedometer, the motor of which had been ruined. The owner of this car had driven from Denver. He was in rather a bewildered frame of mind, but explained that when the engine first started knocking about halfway between Denver and Meade, he had at first thought nothing of it. As more strange noises developed in the motor, and grew louder with distance traveled, he suspected there was something wrong, but kept on going; but even this recklessness is understandable, when you are familiar with a Kansas dust storm. The net result was that by the time he reached

Meade his engine was practically wrecked, and there was no less than a quart of solid dirt in the crankcase.

Actually, I have seen one engine that filled up with dirt while it was standing still, though I would have found this difficult to believe if I had not had the opportunity to examine it with my own eyes. This was a brand-new tractor belonging to a machinery company in business at Meade. They had received shipment of a carload of these engines, and, as they had not enough storage space to accommodate all of them, this one was left outside in the open, where the owners knew it would be exposed to the dust-laden gales, but never suspected that these could cause any trouble with a standing tractor. It stood outside for a week before it was sold, and only when an effort was made to start it was it discovered that the motor was stuck solid. The examination which followed this discovery revealed a condition that was amazing. Everything was filled with dirt. The pistons were wedged in the cylinders so firmly that, after the connecting rods had been loosened, they had to be pounded out. There was only one feasible explanation that could be offered or accepted. The dirt had been blown through the exhaust outlet with such force of wind behind it that it had been driven past the valves into the cylinder, then past the close-fitting pistons into the crankcase.

Even railroad locomotives are not immune to

the destructive action of dust. I have the word of
a master mechanic that after a single trip through
the dust area when the land is blowing, certain
bearings are entirely ground out and have to be
replaced before the engine is again ready for
service. In one case a new locomotive just out of
the shops and on its way out to California where
it was to be put in regular operation, had to be
delayed at Amarillo, Texas, where new bearings
were installed.

There are traffic delays in the Dust Bowl besides
those due to failure of car ignition systems, loss of
visibility during the progress of a black blizzard,
and the ruin of motors when dust reaches the vital
working parts. Frequently the highways are obstructed by dust drifts. Where the roads are lower
than the banks on either side, these cuts will fill
up level with the banks, and it often requires
several days of work on the part of men and trucks
to clear the highway. Railroads are confronted
with the same problems, and occasionally a train is
delayed. Days, and sometimes weeks, are needed
to clear the track completely after a severe dust
storm. Snow plows are quite useless for this work,
and if any other machine more effective has been
invented, I have not heard of it. The dirt has to be
moved mainly by hand shoveling. Snow fences
have been erected along the edges of cuts to keep
the drifting dirt from highways and railroad
tracks. They are effective only until the dirt has

filled in behind them. Then the wind-driven dust goes "over the top" as if the fences were not there.

Airplanes flying over the Dust Bowl during a dust storm used to try to get over the rolling dust clouds, but pilots soon learned that they had to fly either around them or through them. They reported that the atmosphere two or three miles up was still laden with dust. It may be that by now some aviator more daring than the rest has climbed above one of these dust storms, though this is unlikely, and one such undertaking would not necessarily set the altitude limit for all storms.

Electrical phenomena incidental to a black blizzard are many and varied. Lightning and thunder are often continuous and add to the unnerving effect of the storm, particularly in the case of people from happier sections of the country who are experiencing their first dust storm. But even residents of the Dust Bowl feel none too secure. Sometimes a filling station has to be closed down while a storm is at its height, because electricity is running back and forth through the iron pump foundations, which assume a rosy hue. There are very few attendants foolhardy enough to attempt to fill a tank with gas when these conditions prevail.

We have had storms when all the usual means of communication were completely out of commission, including telephone, telegraph, and radio. One of my neighbors who had his aerial hooked direct to his radio, with no ground connections, awoke one night during a storm and was amazed to see his set all lit up in a blinding glare. He was afraid that he might receive a dangerous shock if he touched the wire with his hands. Working with two sticks, he succeeded in disconnecting the aerial, but, with such awkward tools it took him half an hour, during which time the alarming phenomenon continued. Many times, on the blackest of nights, I have glanced out of my window and seen my own aerial, from the house to the windmill and thence to the granary, a line of bright red fire glowing in the darkness.

We who live in the Great Plains don't think much of the kind of country the region has become, yet we are still likely to resent the criticism of a stranger. I am reminded of a tourist from the Pacific Coast who stopped at a service station in Liberal, Kansas. While the attendant was servicing his car, the tourist talked about his trip from the West, and dwelt at some length upon the impressions he had received in driving through the dreaded Death Valley, in California. Then he talked of the part of eastern Colorado and western Kansas he had passed through, and stated with emphasis: "Why, this country is nothing but a desert!"

The filling station attendant, resentful of this remark coming on the heels of the visitor's impressions of Death Valley, retorted: "You went through worse desert back there in California."

"Yes, that is true enough," the tourist agreed, with a smile, "but there aren't any fools out there trying to farm it!"

CHAPTER VII

TRAGEDIES OF DUST

*M*OST of the grim tragedies of the Dust Bowl will never be recorded save in the hearts of near friends and sorrowing relatives. This is partly due to the fact that western Kansas has none but small towns. The only town of any size is Dodge City, and its population is only about ten thousand. This fact of widely scattered, small communities militates against the gathering of anything approaching complete statistics, and no single community cares to advertise itself as worse than its neighbors. However, figures from four small hospitals in the region may prove illuminating. These four institutions reported for the first four months of 1935 that in January 12 per cent of the patients admitted were suffering from acute respiratory infections. In February the percentage admitted suffering from the same condition was 14 per cent. It was 17 per cent in March, and the ratio jumped to 52 per cent in April.

April is usually the worst blow month of the year.

The number of patients admitted to these four hospitals suffering acute respiratory disorders was 233, and 33 of the victims died. That was in

1935. To the same hospitals 115 were admitted in
1934, with 15 deaths, indicating that health breaks
that prevail in the Dust Bowl. Doctors have been
down under prolonged exposure to the conditions
known to state the opinion that mere dust could
hurt no one, but they were not practicing in this
region. The doctors of our region know that dust
endangers the life of anyone whose health is impaired from disease, and that it is often the direct
cause of the deaths of people previously strong and
healthy. There are many victims who, because of
poverty or prejudice, never go to a hospital; and
many patients who are taken there at last by relatives are moribund when admitted, and die within a few hours.

On December 1, 1937, Dr. John H. Blue, of Guymon, Oklahoma, delivered to the Southern Medical
Association a report on fifty-six patients suffering
from "dust" pneumonia whom he had recently examined. In all of them he had found traces of sili-
cosis, which is a disease quite familiar to doctors
practicing in mining communities where certain
types of mining are carried on, or where stone
cutting is an important industry. Rigid scar tissue
develops from the action of the silica particles, and
the disease is classed as incurable. Unless continued exposure is avoided in time, the patient, if
he lives, is very likely to contract tuberculosis.

Silica is described as a body poison which often
affects the digestive organs, the kidneys, the liver,

the circulatory system, and the nervous system, so that many acute infections are likely to develop.

A friend of mine who lived on a farm near Johnson had found himself short-winded for a couple of weeks, but he delayed going to a doctor. He went at last, but only after he found himself without any appetite, fifteen pounds lighter than normal, by the scales, and unable to do any work.

The doctor he consulted is a chiropractor as well as an M. D., and, as he questioned the patient, he was moving his sensitive fingers over his chest. In this way he located a sore spot in one lung. He concentrated his efforts on this organ, while explaining to my friend that, obviously, it had not been functioning for some time. The air tube leading to it was completely filled with dirt, he said, and stated that he had encountered the same condition in no fewer than 367 of his patients that season.

His diagnosis was pretty convincingly confirmed the following day when my friend coughed up several pieces of solid dirt, each three to four inches long and as big around as a lead pencil. The doctor had loosened them by working on the bronchial tube, and my friend was on his way back to the best health that may be expected in the Dust Bowl.

Another case was that of a young man who put off going to see his doctor until it was too late. Though he had just reached voting age and had been a healthy boy, he had been feeling ill for some time. But there was work to be done if the land was to be checked from blowing, so he kept at work listing it, and stuck stubbornly at the task until one evening when he felt so ill that he realized he would have to see his doctor. The physician made an examination and gravely shook his head. "Young man," he gave his verdict, "you are filled up with dust. In my opinion you have only about twenty-four hours of life left to you."

This young fellow had actually been slowly dying on his feet, and lived only twenty-three and a half hours after his visit to the doctor. I have related the circumstances to illustrate that physicians practicing in the Dust Bowl know the effects of dust clogging the lungs, the intestines, and other vital organs. They know that dust kills.

Sad indeed was the case of a farmer and his family living west of Dodge City. It is one of the published cases, and I retell it here for that very reason. It is typical of so many that have not been published, and never will be.

There were four in this little family—a father, mother, and two young children. The elder of the two children died from the effects of dirt, and the day of the funeral was a sad one to the parents. When another black blizzard struck the day after they had laid their first-born in the grave, the young mother began fearing for the life of her one remaining child. She wanted to leave at once, willing to go anywhere just to get out of the dreadful Dust Bowl. The husband also was willing to go; and he went to Dodge City at once, determined to sell his farm at any sacrifice to get money to leave on. But when he reached town and made his mission known, his offer to sell met with grim laughter. No sacrifice he was prepared to make was sacrifice enough. He could not sell at any price, because the prevailing opinion was that the region already was only a desert, and that it could never be classed as farm land.

Discouraged, he returned to his bereaved home. Hearing her husband return, the wife hopefully came running to the door to meet him, leaving the baby in the bedroom, in its crib. She wanted to hear that they could leave.

"Did you sell the farm?" she asked eagerly.

He shook his head dejectedly.

"I couldn't even give it away," he told her.

"Let us go anyway," she urged. "We still have fifty dollars; that will get us somewhere out of the dust."

"Go get the baby, and we'll be on our way," he agreed.

She hastened to the bedroom to get the child, but returned in a moment, weeping and heart-broken.

"There's no use going now," she sobbed. "It is too late. My baby is dead."

This case is typical of many, many tragedies that have occurred and are occurring in the Dust Bowl.

No rifles are fired over new-made graves, no trumpets sound the "Last Post," for these are tragedies of peace, not of war. These are not hero dead, they are merely the victims of dust.

Besides the deaths traceable to the effects of breathing dust there are those, more dramatic, resulting from being caught out in a storm. The black blizzard of April 14, 1935, claimed many victims. One of my neighbors was out in the field driving his tractor when the storm began, and he probably owes his life to clear thinking. When he found himself suddenly in a swirling inferno of dust that blotted out vision and threatened to suffocate him before he could reach shelter, he pulled off his heavy undershirt and soaked it in water from his tractor radiator. Then he covered his face and head with the wet garment and groped his way to a fence that ran directly towards his house. With one hand on the top wire he followed the fence for three quarters of a mile to safety.

Another farmer caught in the same storm had no fence conveniently placed, so he determined to follow a crooked furrow which he knew would lead him home. But the furrow was quickly filled with blow dirt, and it was impossible to follow it on foot. Nevertheless, he made it to the house by crawling on hands and knees, since this humble manner of locomotion enabled him to keep in the furrow by the sense of touch in his hands. He had to crawl a full half mile.

I have mentioned cattle dying from suffocation during some of our worst dust storms. Many have died from the effects of eating dust through being forced to crop the grass too close to the ground in their efforts to pick a scant living from the all but denuded prairies. Many that survived the first one or two blow seasons had to be destroyed anyway, because the dust mixed in the process of chewing their food had ground down their teeth level with the gums.

Living out of cans is no household joke in the Dust Bowl. Sealed cans are the only type of container to which the dust won't penetrate when wind and land are both blowing. Even so, you will have to eat dust with your food if you eat at all while a storm continues, which may mean a period of two or three days. Table and food are covered in the space of a minute or less. Even if you were willing to go hungry for a couple of days, your thirst would compel you to drink; and if you have to go out for a bucket of water while a severe dust storm is raging, the water will be a thin mud before you get back to the house.

Since breathing is unpleasant even indoors while a dust storm is at its height, people sought relief through wearing wet cloths over their faces, during their early experiences with the black blizzards. The cloths soon absorbed so much dirt that they had to be washed out frequently to allow the wearers to continue breathing through the fabric, and this was the usual procedure. But the practice soon proved to be a dangerous one. Persisted in as long as a storm lasted, which usually meant several hours, the constant breathing of damp air, aggravated by the dust, frequently led to pneumonia, with many deaths resulting. Later, the Red Cross introduced a type of dry mask, and now the stores carry these. They are helpful so long as they can be kept fairly free from the clogging dirt, but even the moisture from the breath is enough to form a scum of mud between the mask and the nose or mouth.

There have been occasions at the height of a blow season, when, in the small towns, the residents have not known for days at a time when the sun rose or set. During such periods of prolonged darkness, deaths tend to increase; and days may pass before the dead may be decently buried. In one small community the deaths had mounted to nine before the various sorrowing relatives could venture out to pay their last respects to those who had succumbed.

Do you wonder that week after week during the blow season, the congregations in the churches devote much of their time to imploring the Higher Power to bring to an end the dreaded dust menace? Is it surprising that people who still feel compelled to remain in the Dust Bowl are frequently heard to express themselves in no uncertain terms: "I may live here because I have to. I may die here, because

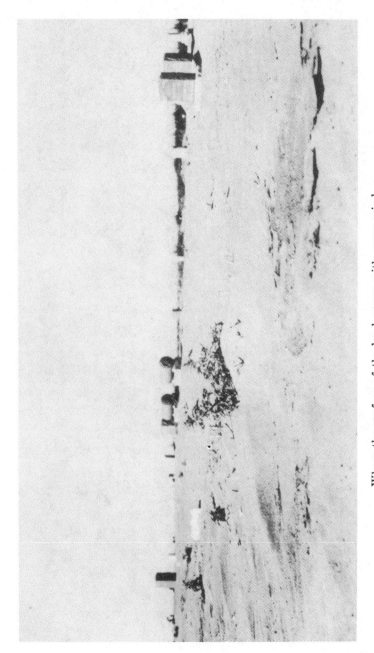

Where the surface of the land moves with every wind—

—even the dead may not rest.

I cannot get away; but God grant me decent burial where the dust never blows!"

Frankly, I share the feeling that here even the dead cannot rest in peace with the dust blowing over their graves—until Judgment Day—in a land where living men and women go insane from the strain, and suicide is too often embraced as the only escape, even by those who dread the consequences of self-destruction in the hereafter.

CHAPTER VIII

BLOW DIRT FARMING

*H*ALF an inch of rain fell near the end of October, and this was enough to help my wheat, but that was the last moisture precipitation we had in 1935, so my crop made very little headway before it froze down for the winter. Nevertheless, despite the late planting and the moisture deficiency, I felt more optimistic about my prospects for a crop than I had the previous year, because of the condition of my land at the time of planting. Part of my wheat was drilled in the maize ground, and if the stalks and roots of maize would help hold my wheat crop when the high winds came in the spring, that would be something to repay me for the labor and money I had expended on the maize I had never harvested. Then I had a quarter section which I had seeded in the ridges, and I felt that this quarter would withstand any gale that might blow.

Out of the northwest, February 3, the first gale of the 1936 season howled down upon western Kansas. From early morning until far into the night it lashed across the face of the land; and though the wind brought a few scattering flakes of snow, any benefit we might have had from this miserly offering of moisture was more than offset by the additional damage done. Driven by the gale, these falling flakes proved a sort of advance guard of destruction. They chiseled out the top of the soil and loosened it up so that the wind might get a better hold on it, thus hastening the always rapid process of wind erosion.

This was one gale that blew itself out without racking my nerves. Perhaps I was learning stoicism and was prepared to accept the worst. Other years, during such a storm, I would have become increasingly uneasy as the hours went by. Every few minutes I would have been looking out the window to see if there was moisture falling that might be expected to check the movement of dust or show that the wind was abating. This time I put in the time sitting at a table reading a magazine, and, though, at frequent intervals, the very house trembled from the force of the gale, I remained undisturbed.

With most of my land better anchored than it had been in other years, because of the roots and stalks of maize, I hardly expected the storm to start any of my soil moving; but even when my confidence proved ill-founded, I found myself hardened to disaster. When, next morning, I drove through and around my fields and discovered that all my land had been blowing with the wind, except the solitary quarter section I had drilled in the ridges, I was more surprised than shocked. The dried maize stalks had been broken off by the wind, and where they had not been completely swept away, they had lodged together in piles over which the dirt now lay a foot deep.

On the road between two of my fields, I stopped in at a neighbor's place, and found that he had not yet been out to see what havoc the gale had wrought.

His greeting was a question: "Well, what's the condition of the crop now?"

"It's like the monkey said when he backed into the lawn mower, 'It's all off now,' " I told him.

He looked at me with surprise, and I was still astounded myself at the change that had come over me. In previous years I would have taken the night's catastrophe very seriously indeed; and here I was joking about it.

The weather remained cold and the ground frozen, but there were no more immediate gales, which was rather unusual for February. In a couple of weeks the weather had moderated and the ground had thawed out; and, in the meantime, I had taken my one-way apart and reassembled it so that it would answer the purpose of a four-row lister. I was ready to start working my land as soon as the ground was in condition to be worked.

There were three quarter sections of land where there were parts that I had left out of wheat under the terms of my allotment contract. These parts I started on first, and ridged up solid. Some of the land that had blown still had wheat on it that was alive, and on this I spaced the ridges, four to a swath, every thirty feet. I did this work to hold the land and to give the wheat a chance to survive; but I knew the winds would probably get all of it eventually, so I did not drive myself as I had in former years. Then my hours had been daylight until dark, whenever there was work to be done; now I worked from about nine in the morning, when the temperature was moderate enough to make working out-of-doors fairly comfortable, until around sundown, when the temperature started going down. When the weather remained too cold for comfort throughout the day, I would not even go to the fields; and I stayed inside the house whenever the dirt was blowing. Even if I only thought it was going to blow, I gave myself the benefit of the doubt and stayed indoors. I had changed my motto from "Never put off till to-morrow what you can do today" to "Never do today what you can put off till tomorrow."

But it was easier to change my mental attitude than it was to make any radical alteration in my habits of life, and I was still getting more work completed than any of my neighbors; but the dust was getting in its deadly work on my constitution and I could no longer bear to be out when a storm was raging. It was the same with many others in the Dust Bowl. The storms of previous years had meant discomfort rather than distress, but the dust had been getting in its deadly work just the same, and the storms had left their mark. A little dust went a long way with these people. To be caught out in the open during even one severe dust storm might very easily prove fatal. That was the way with me. If I stayed in the house while a storm was in progress, it didn't affect me very much, but I did not risk being out in one, if it could by any means be avoided. One afternoon, I was working in the field when a wind came up, and, because it was not very severe, I went on working during the couple of hours or so that it lasted. Its effects made me ill for a week.

The last of my fields that I worked in was in worse condition than any of the rest because of the accumulation of blow dirt on it. This was a field of eighty acres, off by itself, a part of a section of land the rest of which was owned by a near-by neighbor. Back in 1933 I had tried to buy an adjoining eighty acres, without success. I had even offered to pay fifty dollars an acre, though I could have bought similar land at that time for twenty-five. I wanted to own the complete quarter section as a convenient unit for power farming. By this time I was glad that the owner had refused to sell. I doubt if he could have obtained fifteen dollars an acre in 1936 for land I had offered him fifty dollars an acre in 1933.

This eighty-acre field I had planted to maize in 1935, but I had not drilled it to wheat, since its very isolation made it a convenient piece to leave

out of crop to earn allotment benefit. This land
was blowing quite badly, since it had caught so
much dirt from previous years that every slightest
breeze would stir up the dust, and it required only
a light wind to start the soil moving. The north
side of the field had received so much dirt from
the field of the farmer on that side of me, that I
had a drift of blow dirt there two feet deep and
about forty rods long. On the other hand, there
was a tenant farming the land adjoining my
eighty to the south of it, and this fellow had let his
ground blow year after year, to the ruin of my
crops. I had never been successful in persuading
him to check his land from blowing, voluntarily. I
would write to his landlord, who lived at Bucklin,
and in a matter of two or three weeks the tenant
would get busy listing his land; but by that time
my crop on this field would already have been
swept off or buried by the blowing dirt.

There was much blow dirt on this field now, but
all of it, except the drift along the north side, had
come from this man's land. I had the heading of
a draw in this field, and that was filled with six
feet of blow dirt. Close to the road adjoining my
land on the south, there was a bank of dirt four
feet high, forty feet wide, and a quarter of a mile
long. All this had settled on my land through the
neglect and indifference of the same tenant farmer
whose land lay on the other side of the road, and,
now that some of it was being blown back whence

it came, he was mighty anxious for me to get it stopped before it ruined his wheat. He knew better than to come to me with his tale of woe, but I heard about it indirectly, and had to stop that ground anyway, for my own benefit.

But working land in the condition of this field presents special problems to the farmer. In the first place, it cannot be worked when it is even slightly wet, but only when the soil is dry; and even then it is a troublesome job to work it with power machinery, because it offers no solid footing for the tractor. Let the driver wheels spin once and they dig in to the axles and until the rear of the tractor is resting on the ground. Digging out is not so easy. Each time it happened I would have to uncouple the implement, then push a long post under each driver wheel to offer traction to the lugs.

While it is bad enough to have a tractor stall like this in loose blow dirt, you have even more of a job on your hands when a one-way becomes engulfed. The control levers cannot be moved at all, and if they could be moved, they would not help much towards getting the implement out of the ground. I would try dragging the plow out backward, forward, and even sideways. When I was convinced that I couldn't budge it by a steady pull in any direction, then, as a last resort, I would try quick jerks, with the not infrequent result that the log chain would snap. Only when I was sure I could not get the plow out with the tractor would I take to hand digging with a shovel. The problem can be solved by this method, but it means a couple of hours of hard work.

One of my neighbors had a plow so deeply parked under the loose blow dirt that he believed it would have required a whole half day of hand digging to get it free. He had three tractors working in the same field, and with all three of them hooked together, he still had difficulty in dragging the implement from the ground.

With the loose-dirt condition to contend with, the job of ridging the isolated field consumed more than its share of time, and by the time I had finished it, the fields I had first worked over to hold my wheat had started to move again. First the furrows filled up, then the dirt began to blow away, unhampered; but, as yet, my wheat was still alive, so I was determined to hold the land against further blowing if it could be done. If the land was not quickly checked from blowing, the blow dirt would soon kill the crop, so I proceeded to split the ridges, at the same time putting in new ones. This treatment might have held the land against moderate winds, but when another gale struck, everything was destroyed. As the high winds continued, even the land I had seeded in the ridges, which I had felt sure would resist the winds though all the rest should go, at last blew out also, and the ridges filled level. Curiously enough, the gales had no apparent effect on the big blow piles already established. These remained much as they had been since the dirt had been lifted by the wind from adjacent lands and dumped on mine.

None of these succeeding disasters seemed to upset me very much now. I was learning to accept what happened without missing meals or losing sleep; and even when the quarter section which I had expected to hold out against all the winds that could blow went at last like the rest, I still kept on ridging my land so that the soil, at least, might be left to me.

Quite a number of men were employed by the Government for several months taking what might be called a land census in the extensive areas where the land had become subject to blowing. The purpose was to check up on farms that had been vacated by owners or tenants, as well as to record conditions found on the farms that were still occupied or farmed. They wished to determine how much land was being farmed by each owner or tenant; how much of the land that was still being cultivated was land that had deteriorated to such an extent that it could no longer be expected to pay expenses, even under the most favorable seasonable conditions; and how much land, formerly farmed, had lost so much of the topsoil by blowing, that no further attempt was being made to farm it. Of course, what could still be classed as good farming land was also duly recorded as such.

Once again Government funds were available for those who needed supplies to enable them to continue to work their land to check it from blowing; and once again there was a certain amount of chiseling, but the officials responsible for the disbursement of these funds were better informed on the situation of each individual farmer than they had been the year before, so some of the applicants were disappointed. Many of those who had applied for and received financial assistance from the Government for this purpose the year before, were farmers well able to do the work without such aid. This year, when they again applied, they were met with a very rude lecture and a curt denial of funds. Others who needed aid asked for more money than was needed for the actual expense involved in listing their land to prevent the soil from blowing. The amount asked for in their application was scaled down to meet actual requirements. There was one farmer in our region who received Government money from these funds, for the specific purpose which the grant covered; namely, for the purpose of buying supplies to be used in the work of checking the land. But he proceeded to spend it for other purposes. He was very promptly called to account; but when he pleaded that he could not repay the money, and still had no money with which to buy supplies to check his land, the authorities took his situation into account and decided in favor of leniency. They knew he had a wife and two children to support, and that the family, like many others, had suffered privation and hardship, so, instead of ordering prosecution which, under the law, would probably have meant a penitentiary sentence, in the event of the allegations against the man being proved, they gave him a job which enabled him to repay the money he had received from the fund.

CHAPTER IX

A NEW MENACE STRIKES

*W*HEN the blowing season ended for the year about the middle of April, there was more wheat in Meade County than there had been since the bumper crop of 1931. Possibly as much as one fifth of the total acreage that had been seeded in the fall had survived the spring gales, and every farmer was now attempting to forecast his chances of harvesting a crop. The trouble was that no moisture had fallen since October, so what wheat there was was in poor shape, though a sufficient rainfall in time would revive it. Conditions were spotty in the county, some farmers having lost none of their wheat while others had lost all of theirs. I was close to the bottom bracket, having lost all but a hundred acres, which looked now as if it was about to dry up; but the farmers to the west and north of me were still worse off, since, with the exception of the first five miles in these directions, all trace of crop had already vanished. Rain was badly needed, but none came until the twenty-second day of the month, and this was a shower of only three quarters of an inch, which was no more than enough to hold our wheat for a few days. It was the same old gamble of the farmer against the weather, with the latter always having the last word.

Since the greater part of my wheat was already gone, I had to decide what to do with my land in the way of preparing for yet another gamble in the Dust Bowl. Reviewing the different methods of farming I had tried in my efforts to keep my wheat from blowing out: I had seeded wheat in summer-fallowed land; I had drilled in ground that was plowed only once; I had seeded in maize land of one plowing; I had drilled my wheat in maize fields left unplowed; and I had tried seeding in unplowed wheat stubble. My latest attempt to beat the gales had been drilling in the ridges, and it had proved no more certain than any of the rest that I had tried before. My conclusion was that, regardless of how a crop was put in, there was slim chance of getting a harvest unless we got rain in the early part of September so that the wheat would get up in time to make enough growth to protect itself against the wind. Failing that, it would always go with the spring gales.

Having weighed my chances with whatever judgment I had acquired with my experience, I decided not to plant any maize that year, but to summer fallow my land instead. If I cultivated to keep all weeds off and conserve all the moisture in the ground, then, if I did succeed in raising a crop, I might expect it to yield twice as much grain as I would be likely to get from land not summer fallowed. But I was gambling everything on the chance of bringing a wheat crop through to harvest in 1937.

When the weeds are just peeping through the ground, or, to express it more literally, just showing on the surface, the most efficient implement to use is a spring-tooth harrow, and that is what I used to commence with, taking a sixteen-foot swath in my stride and getting over the ground pretty fast. I was able to keep it up with the spring-tooth for nearly a week; but then we had another shower, and the following day, a full inch of rain, which forced me to stop work until the soil had a chance to dry out. By the time it was dry enough to permit me to resume cultivating, the ground I had not been over with the spring-tooth harrow was covered with weeds that were too high for that implement, so I had to use my one-way plow. I went once over every bit of my land except that hundred acres where I still had wheat; and that wheat was looking fine after the rains we had had. I had been all over it by the twentieth of May, when I started back over the land I had worked first; but I had been at it only an hour or so when it commenced raining in earnest Rain fell for two days and nights, with a total precipitation of four inches. But with such a steady rain there was comparatively little run-off into the lagoons. The thirsty earth took it up like a sponge, and it soaked well into the depths of the soil. But the ground remained so soft that it was a week before I could resume my work; and then I had put in only three or four hours when a storm came over that left two inches of water in as many hours, and this delayed my plowing for another two weeks.

As might be supposed, the weeds by this time were thick and still growing fast. They were a foot high all over the field on which I had started work, and as soon as I could begin cultivating again, I put myself on a sunup until dark schedule, because it was very important to kill these weeds as speedily as possible, before they started robbing the soil of its precious moisture.

With this in mind I could not wait for the ground to dry even on the surface. As a matter of fact, it was still pretty wet, and the tractor did a lot of slipping. Occasionally, it bogged down to the axles, so that, with the incidental delays, it took me four days to finish my first field. However, even after this interval, it was just about the time when, ordinarily, I would have been just starting to plow, so I was one big field ahead of my normal schedule. This enabled me to slacken my pace, and I went over my other fields in leisurely fashion, and from then on kept my ground cultivated as it needed it.

The next rain came the fifteenth of June, and I was caught out in it while plowing. It was my birthday, but I would not have needed that fact to remind me of the date, for a mighty downpour lashed by a gale of wind caused the rain to sting and cut like a knife. At the far end of the field, half a mile from my truck, when the water came pouring down by the bucketful, I felt as if the bottom of an ocean had given way over my head, and I was gasping and choking for air. About three inches fell in twenty minutes, so it was not surprising that the surface of the land had disappeared with the deluge, leaving only a vast expanse of water. My wheat prospects on the hundred acres left to me did not look any too good right then, for my crop was leaning rather badly, and, since it was just in the filling stage, I knew that, unless it straightened up, it would not fill well.

However, when I looked over my wheat again, a few days later, most of the straw had straightened up quite well, and the crop was waist high. As I saw it, it looked good for twenty bushels to the acre, and my only regret was that I did not have a lot more like it. In any case, I felt confident that I would not be buying wheat for seed in the coming fall, and that by itself would be more good fortune than had come my way in a long time.

As soon as possible, I was plowing again, trying to get ahead of the weeds which were flourishing after the bountiful rain. I had been at it ten days, and was not far from my truck when I saw a storm coming. I knew if rain came, it would be likely to mean more delay, and I thought I could make another round before the storm hit. I did get about three quarters of the way around, and then down it came, an inch of water in about twenty minutes, so it was not long before the soil was as sticky as mud. I managed to keep the tractor going until I reached my truck, and there I stood like a statue to avoid the clammy touch of my soaking garments, which sent cold chills along my spine every time they came in contact with my skin. I was thinking that we had had more rain that season than at any time since 1930, and that maybe ours was getting to be a wet country. Perhaps the Great Plains country was not doomed to revert to desert after all!

Any farmer who encouraged such dreams of coming prosperity for the Dust Bowl was due to have a rude awakening. The day following the rain we saw the beginning of a new form of calamity, one which we had never previously heard, though it proved to be only a development from what had gone before.

It began with a scorching wind which came from the southwest. No mere breeze this, but more nearly a gale, and it was like a blast from a huge, red-hot furnace. For three consecutive days it blew, slackening at night only to resume each morning as strongly as before; and before that hot blast my prospects for a wheat crop shriveled. Some of the wheat in the region was caught in the bloom, but most of it was in the soft dough stage when the hot winds struck it, and this meant a new form of disaster. The straw and heads turned not yellow, but white, actually cooked by the hot blast. What wheat had not started to fill was now dead; that which was further advanced, and in the dough stage, was left shriveled and light.

So the Dust Bowl had taught us another lesson; namely, that bare ground exposed to the sun will transform warm breezes into fiery blasts. There had been a time when for two or three hundred miles to the southwest of us, a great part of the land no longer being farmed, would in the summertime be covered with weeds. The part that was being farmed would be in maize. Recent years had wrought havoc. Farmers in the region had found it increasingly difficult to hold their land from blowing, and as more and more farmers gave up the struggle and left the land untended, more and more blowing land shifted onto the land of others. Even when unworked land surrounding the remaining farms did not drift on to the cultivated land, it was becoming ever more liable to begin to blow on its own account with every slight breeze that blew. Now came 1936, the year when drouth was laying waste a huge portion of the nation's richest agricultural districts, including the corn states, Missouri and Iowa, and many others that had never known a drouth so severe. Not enough snow or rain had fallen in the southwest to start any vegetation growing, and most of the farmers in the region had vacated, leaving the land to shift with every wind. During the summer months hundreds of square miles of the land were completely bare, unprotected from the sunrays, which they absorbed like fire brick in a kiln, creating the wind which, in turn, brought it to our land, to the destruction of our growing crops.

When the hot wind came I was plowing on land where the weeds were two or three inches high, and though there was an abundance of water in the soil, the weeds promptly wilted. The hot wind seemed to rob all vegetation of its vitality. Personally, I have been in many hot places, including Mexico; but this was my first experience of a wind that caused my face to blister so that the skin peeled off.

Farmers who had seen most of their wheat, or all of it, survive the overwhelming blowing season that spring, found the destruction of their crops by this new menace pouncing out from the unknown a sickening and disheartening experience. Before the coming of the hot wind, their prospects had looked much more favorable than at any time for several years. Many of them were looking forward to their first successful harvest since 1931; and there was another factor that brought additional hardship to some.

These were the farmers who had taken the wrong end of a new form of gamble. In the fall of 1935 a new ruling had come from the AAA which required that, based on the average acreage farmed the three preceding years, only 10 per cent of the total crop acreage would have to be left out in order to enjoy the benefit of a Government allotment. This permitted an increase in the acreage that might be planted to crop in the case of farmers who had reduced their acreage to comply with the allotment terms the previous year, but it did not work that way in the case of those who had always planted their full acreage to crop, because there was still a requirement to be met that the acreage in crop must be at least 15 per cent less than a farmer's total holdings, if a share in the allotment money was to be claimed.

Some of the farmers did not understand about this 15 per cent reduction provision until they went to sign up their allotment contracts in the fore part of June, and it put them in a quandary because they had drilled their wheat in the fall in accordance with their own interpretation of the AAA ruling, and their wheat was now well along, apparently with every prospect of making a good crop. They had their choice of either plowing under part of their wheat or foregoing the allotment money, and it was no easy matter to make a decision. Some had as much as from forty to sixty acres that would have to be plowed under, to comply with the requirements that had to be met if they were to qualify for a share of the allotment, and much of it would yield from twenty to thirty bushels to the acre, provided it survived until harvesttime. That would represent more money than they could collect in allotment checks, so, one way or the other, they had to gamble.

Naturally, they did not all decide the same way. Some chose to take the money and let the extra wheat go; others gave up all idea of collecting allotment money that year, in favor of harvesting their wheat. Those who followed the old adage that "A bird in the hand is worth two in the bush," were, for the most part, the lucky ones. Those who saw their wheat cooked by the hot winds were twice losers; they lost both their crops and the allotment checks they might have had.

Many of these farmers had been so sure of a crop that they had placed orders for new machinery, including tractors and combines; others for new automobiles and trucks. Most of these orders had to be canceled, and the farmer who made his expenses out of his wheat that year, and had enough left for seed, was considered a lucky man. There were a few who harvested their over acreage and still claimed the allotment money, but those administering Government funds were wise to such tricks. The false claimants were caught in their trickery and failed to collect.

Whatever came from the Government, the chiselers were always on the job. The Government had sent out blanks for each farmer to fill out recording, as nearly as practicable, how much crop each of his fields had produced in the years 1926, 1927, 1928, and 1929. These had been good crop years, with the exception of 1927, and some of the farmers figured in their own minds that the new allotment payments would be made on the basis of individual averages instead of on the county average, as before. By the same token, they assumed it was up to them to make the figures good, and some of them turned in reports purporting to show that their land had yielded from twenty to thirty bushels an acre throughout the period under review. One of the farmers selected to look over and check these returns was recognized as one of the best and most successful wheat farmers in Meade County, and his own average for the same period figured out at sixteen bushels to the acre, which included the higher-yielding summer-fallowed wheat. Naturally the boosted figures of other farmers were scaled down, which meant extra work, but was not otherwise important, since the figures had no bearing at all on the disbursement of allotment funds, but were sent to Washington to be filed for future reference.

All in all, the farmers had a hectic year, beginning in June when the United States Supreme Court declared the AAA program unconstitutional. What a turmoil that created! Everybody was wondering if the ruling meant there would be no payments at all in 1936, and banks and oil companies were sharing the farmers' worries. Banks had almost ceased to function as credit-advancing agencies in the Dust Bowl, but they had made some loans. On the other hand, the oil companies had assumed banking functions to the extent of supplying fuel and oil to farmers who could not pay for such supplies, expecting to receive payment when their customers received their allotment checks.

Of course, there was plenty of criticism hurled at the Supreme Court for its decision, most of it unjust and based on self-interest. Some maintained that the decision of the court was merely an attempt to give the New Deal a black eye; others held that questions of politics must have biased the majority opinion; while yet others hinted darkly that money must have been used to influence the ruling of the court. Personally, I felt that the members of our highest tribunal had acted in accordance with their interpretation of the constitution; and I will even go as far as to say that if I had been a member of the court, I would have felt compelled to concur with the majority decision, regardless of how I might have felt towards the needs of the farmers or any of the economic theories involved.

Fortunately for the farmers who had limited their acreage planted in the fall, in the expectation of receiving allotment checks, the Government soon made it known that it had no intention of repudiating its obligations to those who had complied with the AAA rulings in good faith. At the same time it was made known that only the first two-thirds payment would be received on the new contracts, but this was quite acceptable to the farmers who could understand that the Supreme Court ruling had placed the Government in an embarrassing situation. Another method of dealing with the problems involved was to be instituted later.

CHAPTER X

HEAT

ONE OF the hottest summers ever recorded in Kansas was that of 1936. Many areas reported the highest temperatures ever experienced, and there were numerous deaths from the heat. In our part of the Dust Bowl the fleet-footed jack rabbits succumbed and were found dead, scattered over the fields, which was something even the oldest inhabitant had never known to happen before. The jack rabbits had always been considered a nuisance by the farmers, because of the damage done to growing crops. In 1935, they were so numerous that many rabbit drives were organized to get rid of the pests.

These drives attracted a good deal of interest, being photographed and written up for newspapers and magazines. Sometimes a hundred people, men, women, and children, would band together to make a drive, but in the bigger drives as many as two thousand people would participate.

The job of extermination was gone about in a systematic manner that was quite effective. The method was to erect a small corral with wings of woven wire extending for a quarter mile or so from the central pen, the wings forming a giant V.

In the prairie country jackrabbits are rounded up by the thousand, to be shipped to New York for food.

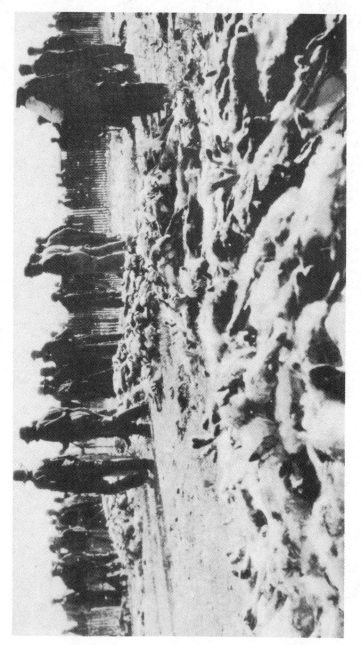

After the slaughter.

Then men, women, and children would encircle an area five miles or more square and begin driving the rabbits towards the center. At first there would be only a few rabbits in sight, bounding along ahead of the beaters, but as the drive closed in, the prairie would be alive with the animals, popping up in every direction, but gradually concentrating towards the trap that had been prepared for them. Once within the wings leading to the pen, many of the jack rabbits seemed to realize what was intended. They would double and twist in their frantic efforts to escape. Some would leap over the line of people hemming them in, only to fall victims to a watchful rear guard. Often as many as five to six thousand jack rabbits were clubbed to death as the result of a single drive; but the meat seldom went to waste, since the kill was usually shipped to the New York market and sold for food.

This course was impractical in the case of millions of rabbits killed in the spring of 1936. There was such a marked shortage of food on the prairies that year that the jack rabbits migrated to the irrigated districts, where they proceeded to eat every green thing in sight, and the farmers in these districts had to take drastic measures to save their crops from utter destruction. They resorted to wholesale poisoning, and millions of jack rabbits were destroyed by this means.

No farmer would think of offering mere heat as an excuse for neglecting the work in his fields. By the first of July, I had finished working over all my land for the second time since the first rain of the year, and my wheat, such as it was, was ready to cut. Harvesting it, however, was no great chore, and the job was done in only two days. My wheat yielded just under four bushels to the acre, and it was poor stuff, shriveled, bleached, and light in weight, since there was little substance to it. Most of it was hull, and since it tested only forty-two pounds to the bushel, it brought a third less than the price of top wheat, which will run sixty pounds to the bushel, or better.

Never before had I seen wheat threshed that weighed less than fifty pounds to the bushel, and threshing such light stuff called for new technique. When the cleaning fans were turned on, the light wheat was promptly blown through the combine and back to the ground, so the force of air had to be greatly reduced, or shut off entirely. This was far from satisfactory, since the result was to throw a lot of straw and chaff in with the grain, but it was the best we could do. Even then, some of the wheat rode over the sieve and was thrown back on the field.

There were a few fields in our neighborhood that yielded around ten bushels to the acre, and there were many that yielded about the same as mine, or between three and four bushels; but some of the fields yielded as low as one bushel an acre, and was hardly worth harvesting.

On the other hand, I know of two fields on which the wheat was an early-maturity variety. This wheat had been in the stiff dough when the hot winds came, and consequently was not nearly so much affected as wheat that had been in the soft dough. These fields produced eighteen bushels to the acre. At first glance it might seem, therefore, that far-sighted farmers would plant more of this early-maturing type of wheat, but the farmer's problem is never as simple of solution as that would suggest. The earlier wheat is likely to be winter killed by the severe cold weather which is an integral part of our usual weather cycle.

There was no letup in the heat immediately following the job of harvesting. In fact, if anything, it continued to get hotter. My policy was to overhaul my tractor twice a season, so that I might feel confident that it would be always in good condition, ready to go and to be depended upon in any emergency that might arise. After harvesting my crop, therefore, I ran my engine into the machine shed and took it apart to grind the valves, replace any parts that were broken or badly worn, put in new piston rings, and generally tune up my mobile power plant.

Heat is my most lasting impression of the afternoon when, having almost completed my overhaul, I was reassembling my tractor. There was not a breath of air stirring, and even with the big doors at either end of my machine shed thrown wide open, it was hot and sultry inside. In order to keep the sweat of my brow from running into my eyes, I was kept busy mopping my forehead, and my clothes were wet from perspiration. Toward the middle of the afternoon, I decided I was thirsty, and proceeded to the house for a drink of water. A dipperful greatly refreshed me, but only until I was halfway back to the machine shed. There I felt an urge to return to the house to have a look at the thermometer that hung on the east side of the house, and was now in the shade. Foolishly, I yielded to the urge, and when I saw that the thermometer registered 117° Fahrenheit, I suddenly felt so thirsty that I had to hurry inside again and drink two more dipperfuls of water.

Nevertheless, work had to go on, and as soon as I had finished reassembling my tractor, I began plowing my stubble. Hardly more than started on it, I was interrupted by a neighbor who was still trying to harvest his wheat. He had three hundred acres that had survived the blowing season but, like mine, had yielded most of its value to the cooking process inflicted by the hot winds from the southwest. He was harvesting only about two bushels to the acre, which would amount to about enough for fall seed, and he was laboring under the handicap that his combine was badly in need of overhauling, particularly the separating unit, which was continually breaking down to delay him.

He was a poor mechanic. He knew very little

about motors, and the two men he had helping him knew even less, so when he came to me asking my help I just had to drop my own work and go with him.

What I found was that he had uncoupled the magneto of the combine motor and could not get it back together again so that the timing would be right. Incidentally, he had reversed two wires leading from the magneto to the spark plugs.

I am rather proud of my own ability as a mechanic, so I did not begrudge the ten minutes it took to have his motor purring smoothly; but my neighbor was back again for help the very next day, and I had to go with him again. This time the carburetor was at fault. I took the carburetor apart which I believe had never been done before for that motor, since some of the jets were actually rusted in. Getting them out, cleaning them, and cleaning the carburetor itself took me between two and three hours. I got the motor running smoothly for the second time, and everything went along all right for a couple of days. Then he was back for the third time, to tell me that the radiator kept boiling every hour or so; and back I went to see what was the matter this time. The trouble was that the bolts linking the magneto to the engine had broken, and in getting the two parts recoupled, he had succeeded in getting the motor timed too slow, which kills power, makes the motor hard to start, and causes it to run hot. This was what was causing the circulating water to boil all the time. Fortunately, after I had corrected the timing, his combine held out until his crop was all harvested, and I was able to go on with my own work without further interruptions from that source.

This business of keeping equipment in good running condition is quite a problem with many farmers, particularly since many successive years of crop failures have discouraged the wasteful practice of junking machinery that should still be in good shape and buying new. My own practice of overhauling my tractor twice in a season is too ambitious or too strenuous for most of my neighbors, though it pays me excellent dividends.

The average farmer is satisfied to overhaul his engine once a year, usually undertaking the job just before starting the season's work in the spring; but money was becoming so scarce in the Dust Bowl that many of my neighbors were seriously neglecting their tractors on which they had to depend for so much of the necessary work they had to do if they were to remain farmers. Those so lacking in mechanical skill that they had to hire the work done were the most seriously handicapped, but some others, who could have undertaken the mechanical work, simply did not have the cash to buy necessary replacement parts. One day I was in a dealer's place of business for some parts I needed, when a heavy-set, middle-aged man came in on a similar errand. I did not know him, but evidently the dealer did. He had the part his customer wanted, but the customer did not have the three dollars, which was the second-hand price. That was a pretty small sum for a farmer needing a part for his tractor, but that farmer asked for credit. He wanted to pay for the part when he received his allotment money from the Government, and when the dealer refused, on the ground of a company rule requiring the payment of cash for parts, he went out without the part he needed.

This being the financial straits in which many farmers found themselves, it has become more and more a common practice over a period of two or three years to keep a tractor running just as long as it would hang together. When the engine stopped, the owner would make such replacements as were absolutely necessary to get it running again, and second-hand parts were certainly preferred if they could be obtained. After the tractor had been thrown together again, it might continue to run for a day, or a week, before some other vital part gave out. Then it had to be torn down again, and that part replaced.

Of course, such serious neglect of valuable machinery is costly. A tractor that is not properly maintained will run itself into a state of dilapidation within a couple of years, while the constantly recurring necessity for small repairs will in the aggregate prove easily twice as expensive as a general overhaul given regularly each year.

Moreover, running a heavy machine like a tractor in a condition of disrepair is dangerous to the operator. One of my acquaintances had a narrow escape from death when an engine broke down suddenly, and so seriously that it flew into hundreds of metal fragments.

But, often, the owners of these neglected tractors are doing the best they can in their circumstances of financial stringency. They have no money and can borrow none, so they make what repairs they can, and hope against hope that their engines will hang together until a season's work is finished. Maybe they will harvest a decent crop next summer; and if they do, and the market yields them a fair price, the profit will enable them to recoup their fortunes and buy a new tractor. Unfortunately it has not worked out that way for many of them.

In spite of interruptions from my neighbor with the crippled combine, I finished working over my stubble ground. The day I completed the job I pulled over to a part of the quarter section where there were a few scattered weeds that had not been killed by the previous plowing. While I worked, I could see a foaming black cloud of dirt fogging up eastward of me, but I gave it no particular attention until one of my neighbors came over to tell me that part of my land was contributing to that dust cloud. I drove my tractor over there as quickly as possible, for I had to get the field checked at once. My experience has been that if a piece of land starts blowing in midsummer, it is likely to prove a continuing source of trouble, being quite likely to start blowing again in the fall as soon as the soil has been loosened up by drilling. That is why I stopped plowing at once, hooked my tractor to the spring-tooth harrow, and moved over to the quarter section that was blowing. I stayed with the job until I had gone over the entire quarter, and found that I could still work with a will, if I thought the occasion demanded it.

When I had stopped my land from blowing, I went back to plowing where I had left off, and, since by that time a fresh crop of weeds had sprung up all over my summer-fallowed ground, I kept on plowing, while, day after day, the sun continued to beat down relentlessly, with never a breeze stirring. Morning after morning I was at work in the field when the sun came up, but already wishing it was quitting time. When starting the tractor after lunch, I would have to throw a gunny sack over the crank before I could take hold of it. Heat from the engine made even breathing almost unbearable, while gnats and other torturing insects added to the general feeling of misery. It was so hot that cold water poured on metal exposed to the sun would sizzle and cloud up in steam.

Since this was the last time I would have to work my land before drilling in my wheat, I had plenty of time to do the necessary work. Always before, in our section of the state, summer nights had been cool enough to sleep under some covers; but in the summer of 1936 the nights were so hot that everybody complained about being unable to sleep. All the night through the thermometer would hover in the upper eighties, or even in the nineties, and there was one night when it registered one hundred degrees at midnight, and held there until morning. So, with no need to rush my work, I was glad to quit for the day every afternoon between five and six. What little relief there was to be had from the heat was in the early mornings during the first two or three hours of daylight, when it usually remained comparatively cool. That was why I daily met the rising sun.

It was early in August when I finished working my land, and I believed I had reason to be satisfied with the plan I had decided on; namely, to summer fallow my land, instead of planting maize or any other crop prior to seeding my wheat in the fall. Other farmers had planted maize and had had no greater fortune with it than I had had other years. Having been exposed to the hot winds, with no rain in over a month, it promised very little in the way of a crop, and of course it had drawn moisture from the soil. I had four feet of moisture in the subsoil, which was more than I had had in six years, and more than any of my neighbors had, so I felt that I had an excellent chance to get my wheat crop well started, and to harvest a fine crop in 1937.

CHAPTER XI

DUST SICKNESS

SINCE the United States Supreme Court had declared the AAA unconstitutional, the stalwarts of the administration had been racking their brains in an effort to evolve some method of farm control that would justify continuing payments to the farmers. Those at the helm felt that money was needed to keep up morale among the farmers and to insure that they would be disposed to continue their co-operation with Government agencies when a new farm program was established. So far as the farmers in Meade County were concerned, no one need have worried about our willingness to co-operate. We needed no persuading to grasp at anything that seemed to promise returns, regardless of either political or economic technicalities.

Nevertheless, preliminary announcements regarding the new policy were to some extent confusing, since it seemed to tend in a direction opposite from that of the former crop-reducing program. Conservation was the keynote of the new farm-policy tune, and future payments depended upon the farmer's agreeing to cultivate a specified acreage by methods which would almost double the average production of wheat. In June I had signed a Government contract, under which I certified that I was summer fallowing the 15 per cent of my acreage that had to be left out of crop in order to comply with the 1936 farm program, and in return would receive payment for this co-operation without reference to future co-operation by way of acreage reductions in accordance with future farm programs. When seeding time came we had no definite information about the terms of the 1937 allotment policy, except that 20 per cent of the average acreage would have to be held out of crop in order to participate. For my part, I felt that I was making my last stand in the Dust Bowl. If I failed to harvest a crop in 1937, everything I had would be gone, and I would have no further interest in Government farm programs of any kind. I had summer fallowed all the land under my control and I decided to put it all in wheat; and I knew that I had to get my seed in the ground and my wheat up early in September, or face the probability that it would all blow out again.

When a shower brought us a half inch of rain on the third day of September, I began drilling wheat. The rain was not sufficient to penetrate the loosened topsoil to the moisture below, but I felt that I had to take a chance. Two of my neighbors followed my example, but everybody else held back. Most of them had procured their seed from the elevators, either by promising to pay for it when they received their next allotment checks, or by mortgaging their 1937 crop. If that seed was lost from lack of sufficient moisture to bring it up, they would not be able to replace it.

Following my own decision, I drilled for four days, and in that period seeded four hundred acres. I had started on the part of my land that was most likely to blow if unfavorable conditions continued to prevail so I realized that if I had been premature with my seeding, the mistake was likely to prove a costly one. On the other hand, if we did get sufficient moisture to start my wheat, the early drilling would mean a better chance to get that part of my land firmly anchored in advance of the blowing season.

However, I was now willing to wait a few days to see what this wheat would do, before going ahead with the drilling of the rest of my land. The story was soon told, for the summer heat continued and the ground dried out to below the depth of the sown wheat so rapidly that most of my seed failed to sprout. When wheat lies in dry soil, the wireworms, which have always been present these later years, destroy the kernels by eating the hearts out of them. The plants that did come up on my land served only to provide succulent pasturage for a horde of grasshoppers which ate the green sprouts almost as fast as they came to the surface; and once again I was loser in a gamble with the elements. Maybe I had been lucky in delaying the drilling of the rest of my land, but I cannot be sure even of that, because the two of my neighbors who had drilled at the time I did soon had a good stand of wheat which the grasshoppers were not bothering at all. So far, they were ahead in their gamble with nature.

There now began for me the toughest fight of all my experience in the Dust Bowl. Perhaps the conditions I had to battle against were no worse than I had had to contend with in other seasons, but they were complicated by a period of illness, brought on by the havoc that successive blowing periods had wrought on my constitution.

First of all, I had to buy wheat to replace the seed I had lost. There was a scarcity, and I had to pay a premium above the market quotations to get what I needed. My seed cost me $1.15 a bushel; but I got my supply, then waited for rain.

Sunday afternoon, the twenty-seventh of September, low-hanging, heavy dark clouds formed and floated overhead, but I was by no means certain they spelled the rain my land so badly needed, even when a drizzle began to fall. I recall that a neighbor came over to tell me that his truck was out of working condition, and to ask me to haul a load of coal for him, and that, in the course of our conversation, I had told him that if rain did not come by the end of the month, I would drill no more wheat, but would sell out and look for a new location somewhere outside the Dust Bowl.

But even while we talked, the misty drizzle was

becoming more dense, and my friend cut short his visit to go home for shelter. Soon it began to rain in earnest, continuing far into the night, drenching the land with an inch and a half of precipitation, which meant fresh encouragement when I sorely needed it.

Thus, the first of October found me again hard at work drilling wheat, and while I made slow progress in the wet ground, I had the satisfaction of knowing that drilling in such ground would, to some extent, reduce the blowing hazard. Besides, with so much ground to go over, time was of the utmost importance. A few days of delay might make a great deal of difference in my chances for a crop, so it was up to me to give my wheat as early a start as was now possible.

But this was one of those times when I was due to get more rain than I needed. The third day after I started drilling, a shower came about sundown, and, with a half inch of precipitation, it was heavy enough to halt operations. However, since the weather had been threatening all afternoon, and the next day was Sunday, I was glad the rain had held off as long as it had, and was not much delayed in my work. On Monday morning I was drilling again before the sun made its appearance, and kept at it until long after darkness had descended; but when it rained almost an inch that night, I began to feel dismayed.

One of my neighbors had his wheat up and growing, so I made a deal with him to drill part of my land, which he agreed to do as soon as the ground was dry enough for the work of seeding to be resumed. This time I was delayed by another shower, and it was Saturday afternoon before I could resume drilling where I had left off Monday night. The ground was still so wet that I had to unhook one drill, because one was all my tractor could pull in the heavy ground. This made slow work of it, but because it was so late in the season I could not afford to wait for the ground to dry sufficiently for normal drilling operation, though naturally the neighbor I had hired to help did not feel so anxious as I did. He promised to start Monday, if there was no more rain in the meantime.

Except when harvesting wheat, or in some emergency, I have never made it a practice to labor on the Sabbath, but I was now in no position to choose my working days. I kept going all day Sunday with my one drill. On Monday morning the ground was dry enough so that I could couple on the second drill, and, with the hired outfit starting at the same time, we began to make good time in getting over the ground. We finished drilling the fourteenth of October, and, with mild weather continuing to prevail, my wheat came up and made a fair showing. It had been seeded too late to obtain as much growth as I should have liked to see before it froze down in December, but I felt fairly confident that it would hold its own through the spring blowing season. At least I had done everything in my power to assure a wheat crop, and I felt fairly well satisfied. The weather ahead was something I could neither foresee nor control.

We had a good snow in January, and if it had remained on the ground until spring, it would have been a wonderful help in protecting the wheat from blowing when the winds came. This, however, was too much to hope for, and the snow was soon followed by a warm sun which speedily melted the white blanket that had so briefly covered the earth. When the first gale came, on the fourth of February, it caught the land without any protective covering except the growing crops, and some of my wheat was too immature to withstand even the first wind. A small patch of about two acres in extent started moving in a corner of one of my fields, and I well knew that if I did not get it stopped at once the next wind would speedily ruin the whole field, though the ground was frozen to within three or four inches of the surface. Instead of holding the land, the frozen condition increased the difficulty of working it. The only implement I could use was a spring-tooth harrow, and in order to make that effective I had to remove most of the teeth. But, with only sixteen teeth, spaced a foot apart, I was able to tear up large clods of frozen ground, which left the surface rough to resist the wind.

Nevertheless, I was worried about a big bank of blow dirt that had accumulated along the north side of that field during the previous summer. If I tore that up with the spring-tooth harrow, it would move all the sooner when the frost went out of the ground, whereas, if I waited until that happened, going over it with my lister would hold it for a while. Since the surface had thawed out, this bank was already on the verge of moving, but there was nothing much I could do until the thawing-out process had penetrated to a greater depth.

Several dusters swept over my land before the middle of February, but none of them was severe enough to do any particular harm. All I had to do was to watch my land, so that I would be ready to check at once any ground that showed signs of blowing. But I lived in constant anxiety in case one of the more ferocious gales experienced in former years should come, for I feared the effects might prove disastrous; and, sure enough, one of these struck the twentieth of the month, and at two o'clock in the morning, when there was nothing I could do about it immediately.

After the wind began to howl, sleep was out of the question for me. I kept thinking about the dirt bank lying out there in the inky blackness. If it started moving, it would probably spell ruin to that entire field of the best wheat I had; but if it held until dawn, I might yet be able to check it in time.

Before the first suggestion of light appeared in the eastern sky, I was ready to start to cover the two and a half miles distance to this field. Despite plenty of heavy clothing, the wind cut through me like a knife, but I had far too much at stake to hesitate, and I reached the bank only in the nick of time, since it was actually beginning to blow when I reached my objective.

If I dug into the frozen ground beneath the loose soil that was beginning to blow, it would mean breaking my lister to pieces, so I eased the implement into the ground as far as I dared, and pulled ahead. My lister did not break, and it took me only about an hour to list the entire bank, but I was suffering so intensely from the penetrating cold that it was just about the longest hour of my life.

With a sense of relief and satisfaction I started for home. I felt as if I were all but frozen stiff, but I knew I would soon thaw out before a roaring fire. But I was only part of the way home when I came upon another of my fields in distress. There were a couple of spots out in the middle of the quarter section that were just starting to blow, and, of course, they had to be stopped. Checking these two small areas would have been speedily accomplished, but I had no more than pulled into the field to start the job when my tractor broke down—just when I so desperately needed it. A valve stem had snapped off, and I viewed the damage with dismay, because I knew that a snapped valve stem usually means ruin to the block and assembly, including the cylinder head, and a repair job requiring two days at least.

Certainly I had no stomach for the job of pulling my engine apart exposed to the bitter cold and flying dust; and to do so would be of no advantage to my blowing land. The wind was increasing, and another day would see the whole quarter section blowing and ruined completely so far as the present crop was concerned. That land simply had to be checked without any unnecessary delay.

Since my tractor had broken down, I had to walk home; and half an hour before a hot fire took the chill out of my bones, during which process I decided that I would have to borrow a tractor from a neighbor. This decision was made only reluctantly, for I had always prided myself on my self-reliance; but this was one time when I would have to put my pride in my pocket, or lose a lot of my wheat.

My neighbor's wheat had started to blow as badly as mine, or worse, but he had no intention of trying to stop it while the dust blew and the temperature remained so bitterly cold; so when I told him I wanted to borrow his engine so that I could check my land, he consented to let me have it with the utmost cheerfulness.

As a matter of fact, his tractor had not been run since fall. Moisture had got into the cylinders through the exhaust pipe, and they were full of water, which made starting the motor a back-breaking job. I was cold again when I started cranking, but the more I cranked the warmer I became, so that, by the time I had the engine roaring, I had most of my clothes off, and was still perspiring.

I reached my field none too soon. Where there had been two spots blowing, one fourth of the entire field was now affected and on the move, so I lost no further time in getting my lister into the ground. Time was too valuable for me to stop for dinner, so I kept going all afternoon, while the gale continued until dark, though, fortunately, the temperature moderated after midday.

When I returned the borrowed tractor to its owner that night, I felt that I had earned the right to feel optimistic. I had checked my land from blowing, and my wheat had suffered no great damage. By doing what had to be done in face of bitter wind and swirling dust, I felt as if I had conquered the dust menace, and could do it again, which made the future of my crop seem secure.

But I did not sleep well that night, for the dust I had labored in all day began to show its effects on my system. My head ached, my stomach was upset, and my lungs were oppressed and felt as if they must contain a ton of fine dirt.

In the morning my inclination was to remain in bed, but outside there was another gale blowing, and it was fiercer than that of the day before.

Probably some of my wheat was already blowing, but I knew it would be suicidal for me to go out while that dust storm was at its height, so I waited impatiently for a letup. Around noon, the fierce wind slackened, and I drove in my truck out to the field where I had left my tractor. If my land was blowing, there was nothing I could do about it until I had repaired my engine, unless I borrowed my neighbor's tractor again, which I did not want to do. I kept my eyes averted from my fields, so that I could not see how badly they might be blowing.

This was one time when the reality proved to be less than the trouble I had anticipated. Within a half an hour I had the cylinder head off my motor, and then I found, to my very great relief, that the valve stem had only been bent by the plunging piston. All I would have to do to have my engine running again would be to replace the valve and guide, which meant considerably less of a job than I had expected.

By sundown I had my tractor ready to go, and I decided to make an early start next morning. It was barely light when I headed for my fields. The wind was blowing from the south, and, while there was no dust in the air as yet, I knew the wind would be a gale by noon, with swirling dirt obscuring the whole landscape. So, when I discovered that some twenty acres in one of my fields had been blowing the day before, I started on that at once, because I knew if I did not get it checked before the wind became a duster, I would be likely to lose not only this field, but two others lying directly north of it, which would likely be affected by its blowing.

My good intentions received a setback almost as soon as I started to give effect to them. On my very first round of the moving area, I made a turn too close to a little-used road. As a result, I struck among some weeds where the ground was still frozen, and the shock snapped the beam of my lister, which put it out of commission for the time being.

I could have used my one-way, if it had been converted for listing, but that had not been done, and there was no time to do it now, while my land lay at the mercy of the wind. The only thing I could do was to go home for my spring-tooth harrow. That would not be very effective in holding the land, but it would hold it temporarily, which would give me time to repair my lister, or re-arrange the discs on my one-way plow.

So home I went for the spring-tooth, and by the time I reached the field again, the wind had risen. Nevertheless, I was determined to check the blowing of my land, even if I had blindly to grope my way through driving dust to get it done.

When I finished the job of stopping my land, I returned to the house so filled up with dust that I could not eat, and I stayed indoors until afternoon merged into evening, then into night—a sleepless night during which I ran a high fever, and felt as if I must be on the inside of a volcano.

When morning broke, the wind was still blowing; but I staggered out to see how my land was faring. The area I had gone over with the spring-tooth harrow the day before was already moving again, and the dirt from it was blowing onto adjacent ground, chiseling away at the soil till it too threatened to go, and burying my fine wheat. The ground had to be checked again, and quickly, or three quarter sections of crop would speedily be destroyed.

My spring-tooth was still the only implement I had available for the work, but I thought I could make it effective. By sinking the teeth of the harrow as deeply into the ground as they could be adjusted to penetrate, I succeeded in bringing up new clods to hold and anchor the pulverized topsoil. This was doing the work all right, but it was a terrific drag on the tractor. When I found I could not pull the load in high, I tried it in low, but this made my progress much too slow. The blowing area was already spreading, and I could see that I could never hope to catch up with the forces of destruction at such a snail's pace. Besides, I was ill, and it was dangerous to me to be out in that storm any longer than was absolutely necessary. There was only one thing to do, and I did it. I opened up the governor to increase the engine's power and traveling speed, and this enabled me to pull the load in high. This was putting an excessive strain on the motor, and I was well aware that I could not expect the engine to stand up under it for long; but I had my tractor walking at six miles an hour, or two miles over its rated speed, despite the excess load, and all I asked of it was that it hold together until I had checked my land and anchored it against the destroying wind.

If the engine was laboring against an intolerable load, so was I. Dust was coming into my system through my mouth as well as my nostrils, and I was choking, wheezing, and gasping for air. My eyes were filled with dirt and they hurt painfully; but when every little while I found myself completely blind, with my eyes wide open, empty blackness engulfing me, I knew that this was not caused by dirt. I was hovering on the verge of unconsciousness, but fought off these spells, with the thought that if I fell it would mean almost certain death. The drivers, half filled with wet earth which kept the lugs from penetrating to obtain complete traction, would occasionally slip as they struck a spot where all the loose topsoil had already blown away. The resulting jolts threatened to tear the head from my body but they helped to keep me conscious, too, and I stuck with the job long after I had completely lost track of time. I held to the thought that this land had to be stopped from blowing, and I kept driving on and on.

Later, I estimated the ground I had gone over at

fifty acres, from which I judged that I must have
finished it about noon. But I have no recollection
of finishing that field, nor of how or when I got
home. I believe I must have been delirious. It was
four o'clock in the afternoon before I began to
realize that I was in my own house and that the
world was still rolling along on its appointed
course, even as the wind was still howling and
wailing outside.

My condition had been bad enough that morning,
but now it was complicated by a cold that con-
gested my lungs. I began to wonder just what
benefit a successful wheat crop would be to me, if
I gave up my life in the attempt to save it from
the elements. Whatever happened, I was now
forced to stay in the house, where I should have
been from the beginning of my illness. In doctoring
myself I must have used enough liniment to float
a battleship, but it gave me relief; and when the
gale slackened next day, I could at least breathe
clean air again. We counted our blessings as they
came.

However, I was still a pretty sick man, feeling a
little better one day, and a whole lot worse the next,
until after four days I reached a crisis in my illness, and doubted if I could pull through. A neighbor who knew my condition came in that afternoon
to see if there was anything he could do for me.
There was nothing he or anyone else could have
done for me just then, and I told him so; but I

asked him to look in on me the next day to see if I had lived through the night.

That was one night when, I believe, the issue of life or death for me depended on the elements. If the wind had gone on the rampage again and raised a lot of dust, I probably would not have lived through it; but there was no wind, and there was no dust, and I held my own.

Taking me at my word, which I had meant in all sincerity, my friend came over next morning. The crisis was over, and I was on the mend. In a couple of weeks I was on my feet, and if I had lost twenty pounds in weight, that was something I was likely soon to get back.

CHAPTER XII

IF I SHOULD LEAVE THE DUST BOWL

*M*ARCH came in like a lamb in our part of the Dust Bowl. Soggy, moisture-laden snow fell the beginning of the month, and it melted quickly, so that it soaked through the topsoil and met the moisture that still lay in the subsoil. True, there were still frequent winds, but they were milder winds, both in strength and duration. Until well along in the month none of them lasted over a day. With warmer weather the wheat was beginning to grow, and the thermometer of my hopes began to climb steadily upward. On the ground that I had gone over once with the spring-tooth harrow, my wheat was coming along splendidly, with the stand showing very little thinning as the result of the extra working the ground had received. Even the ground I had ripped over twice with the spring-tooth had what I estimated at a half stand— enough to make a fair crop yield, if only favorable conditions might continue.

But on the twenty-third of the month a fierce gale out of the southwest unleashed itself, and, south and west of me, all signs of crop were speedily wiped out. I have told of my experiences in the dust storm that followed, when I agreed to drive for a friend who had an important errand, and how we reached home at last by following the directions given us by a road worker caught out in the same storm. By the time we reached home the wind had slackened, if you remember; but at two o'clock the following morning another gale sprang up. This one was from the northwest, and it has been recorded as the fiercest gale in the history of Kansas. The wind reached a velocity of fifty-two miles an hour, and never before in any wind had my house shaken and trembled so continuously.

Daylight came, and the wind was still blowing at its height, and I dared not venture out into the swirling dust which had done away with all visibility. Vividly before my eyes I pictured my wheat crop hanging in the balance. Some of it had doubtless been ruined in the night, but I was confident that most of it yet survived. If only the wind would slacken now, I would yet have a crop, but if the gale continued until noon, I could see no hope for my wheat.

It continued to blow until noon and long after; and the thermometer of my hopes reached a new low, for now I saw all of my crop gone, and I felt utterly discouraged and sick at heart. No longer was there need for me to care how long or how hard the wind might blow, since whereas, only yesterday, I had considered my prospects brighter than they had ever been since first I had started to farm in the Dust Bowl, there was now nothing left for me but to give up, accept utter defeat, and move away from western Kansas.

I was fortunate that I had a little money on hand. About a week before I had received from the Government a check representing 90 per cent of the money due me because I had summer fallowed part of my land held out of crop the previous year. No more than half of what I would have received for a season under the now outlawed AAA, it was still a nest egg. I could not have put out another crop with it, if I had wanted to, but it would have paid my way to any part of the country where I might have desired to settle, and it would have supported me in comfort until I could have found employment.

At ten o'clock that night the wind died down, and, after I had taken my bedclothes out-of-doors to shake them free of most of the dust that filled them, I went to bed and slept. Next morning, I awoke to find the sun shining brightly, a gentle breeze blowing, a few jack rabbits out jumping around, and the birds cheerfully chirping. As long as you kept your gaze skyward, it was hard to believe that the worst gale in Kansas history had so recently ceased; but there were chunks of coal as big as hens' eggs scattered over the yard, blown from an open pile near the house, and, as far as I could see, my fields had been denuded, all my wheat gone.

There was no need that I could see to go further

afield to mourn over my distant acres, so I prepared breakfast, and, while eating, began considering the prospects in distant states. If I was going to make a fresh start in life, then the sooner I got away from the Dust Bowl, the sooner I would be on my way to a new life. A neighbor who farmed land that adjoins mine came in to compare notes. He had been out looking over the ruins of his field, and as he opened the door my first words were: "How is it? All of my wheat is gone, isn't it?"

"No, not quite all," he told me, and you may well believe I pricked up my ears. "The quarter section over northeast of here has come through in pretty good shape."

My hopes began to rise once more, for I knew my neighbor had passed four of my fields on the way, and he was as well qualified as I to estimate the prospects of the field he had mentioned. If that quarter section had survived the terrific punishment of the previous day's gale, then, perhaps I was not through after all. If conditions remained favorable from now on, that quarter might produce four or five thousand bushels of wheat. That would be enough to tide me over another year, and would enable me to put in another crop.

With my checkered fortunes presenting a new prospect I had to go out to see for myself just what my prospects might be, and what I saw decided me to keep on fighting for a while, at least. There was that one quarter section of wheat that had held its own against the wind and survived, and there was another field where my wheat had held out, though badly damaged by the dirt from another man's field, which had moved in on it. My other fields were in the condition of ruin I had expected to find prevailing over all my land. In many places the wheat had turned white, indicating that it was already dead, while in other places the loose soil had been swept away, to leave the plants dangling in the air, anchored only by the main tap roots. Even the crop planted in the previous year's stubble had all blown away; and never before had I seen so much dirt moved by one wind. The blowing of one field had filled up a deep ditch that had been recently excavated in the making of an improved road. It had jumped the road and filled the ditch on the other side of it, bank full, then had drifted into the field lying to the south of the road.

As I finished my survey of my fields I came to the conclusion that the only crop I had left was the wheat in the lone quarter section that had held its own. There was not over one chance in a hundred that strip listing might prove effective in checking my other fields from further blowing; but I could not bring myself to leave my farm so long as I had that one quarter of wheat. I had plenty of time on my hands while awaiting the final outcome, so I decided to work my land again as soon as the weather became a bit more pleasant.

While waiting I had the opportunity to see what

the big wind had done elsewhere than on my land, and it had done plenty of damage. Besides destroying crops it had totally wrecked many buildings throughout the area. Many farmers had empty steel grain bins of one thousand bushels capacity, and the gale seemed to have shown a preference for these as objects of its fury. Many were torn from their moorings, and demolished, and those that could not be torn loose from their moorings, had their sides caved in, or their tops ripped off, or both. One of these grain bins had been set between four long, well-anchored poles, too strong to be snapped off; but the wind had lifted the bin clear of the poles, then completely wrecked it.

Following my decision to do what I could to check my land and salvage what little of my crop might yet be salvaged, in a couple of days I commenced going over the ground that had blown, using a single-row lister. I was starting on ground that had trapped much dust from adjacent land, and I had very little faith in the work I was doing, since I was certain that one wind would start it moving again. I dug the implement in as far as it would go, so that the beam itself was dragging on the surface. This was the deepest I had ever seen a lister go, measuring two feet from the bottom of the furrow to the top of the half ridges. Spacing the furrows thirty feet apart, I kept on working, for I had always made a practice of struggling against all odds, and, as long as I remained in the Dust Bowl, I was determined to maintain that reputation. Only time and nature could decide the ultimate fate of my remaining good quarter, and it was easier to work than to remain idle pending the decision.

While I was making the last round on my south field and was plowing close to the road, the man farming the other three quarters of the same section came over to talk. I had seen him wandering in aimless fashion over his land, and evidently he had been trying to make up his mind whether or not to start work on it. Anyway, that was what he wanted to ask my opinion about. He said his wheat was still alive and would be all right if no more winds came, and he wanted to know what I thought he should do about it.

My own example should have been answer enough, but I realized that if his land began to blow again it would soon put the finishing touches to my own already badly damaged field, so it was as much in my own interest as his that I advised him to check his land.

The rest of his conversation I found grimly amusing. We happened to be alongside a big dirt drift forty rods long, forty feet wide, and four feet high, and all of that dirt had come from his land to mine. Moreover, he was the same man who, year after year, had permitted his land to blow unchecked, reckless of the havoc wrought with the crops of others all around him; but now he was talking about there being so much blow dirt on his land that he could not cope with it, and he laid the blame on the fact that everybody else's land was blowing in on his, which statement was intended to include mine.

I had heard it said that if a man tells a lie often enough, he may come to believe it himself, but this was my first personal experience of such a curious condition of mind. I smiled, but said nothing in reply.

Since the blowing season was not yet over, the winds soon resumed, after our brief spell of quiet; but the strongest of them was nothing compared with the great gale that had almost completely destroyed my crop. I took a fresh grasp on hope when, to my surprise, my land seemed to be holding; but these hopes were quickly dashed, not by my land moving this time, but from another cause. Only now was the secondary effect of the big blow becoming apparent. The electricity generated by the driving dust had affected my wheat in a manner I had not previously seen, and my wheat was looking worse than ever. Even on my one good quarter a lot of the foliage had withered and died since the storm, and it looked as if nature's decision had already been given, since my crop seemed doomed to be a total failure.

There were some of my neighbors who offered encouragement. They said that wheat in the condition mine was would recuperate and be as good as ever, but I knew they were guessing blindly, since they had had no more experience of that condition than I had had—and that was none. Though I had no intention of giving up until I was quite sure that my last hope for a crop was gone, I resumed planning for the future, with the thought of getting away from the Dust Bowl uppermost in my mind.

While it looked as if I would have to go, I was hopeful that I might not have to rely entirely on the Government money I have mentioned as a nest egg. I had recalled a friend of mine living in the sand hills twenty miles north of me, and that he had once told me that if I decided to vacate my land, he would like to take it over and farm it. Now I decided to drive over and see him, on the chance that we might be able to arrive at a satisfactory deal.

When I reached his home I found only his wife there. She informed me that her husband was at work, listing his land, in a field that was several miles from their home, and she gave me instructions how to reach him. Either these instructions were not quite clear, or else I misunderstood them, for, where I expected to find my friend, there was no one in sight. Later, I was not disappointed that things fell out this way, for in my search for him, I had an opportunity to observe conditions in a part of the Dust Bowl other than my own.

I drove on, and stopped at the first house I came

A combine after a dust storm.

Farm machinery buried by dirt.

A machinery sales building that has not been used for years.

Not since 1931 have these combines been put to work.

Colossal elevator that has had little grain in it since 1931.

to, in the expectation of receiving new directions. The house was vacant. Most of the roads were blocked by huge dunes of drifted sand, but there was another house about two miles from the first, and I started out in its general direction. After making two wide detours to avoid the sand drifts, I reached the place. These detours had taken me through a big field where my car had once sunk to the axles, so you may be sure I was glad to reach my immediate destination. All the greater, therefore, was my disappointment when I found that this house also had been vacated, though there were signs of recent occupation which told me that the family that had occupied it had only recently pulled up stakes and left. The third house I reached was inhabited, but it seemed that the owner would be unable to help me in my quest, until he suddenly remembered that the occupant of yet another house, down the road a way, was a brother-in-law of the man I wanted to see.

When I reached the fourth house, I told the man I found there, by way of introduction, that I had shucked corn for his brother-in-law in 1926. This served to break the ice. He asked my name, and when I gave it, he said that while he had never met me before, he knew all about me; and I had the satisfaction of knowing that the reputation I had made as a lad of eighteen was still remembered.

My new acquaintance related some of his own experiences in the Dust Bowl, and he was even more discouraged than I was. He told me that in 1931 he had raised thirty thousand bushels of corn but had sold it for only twenty cents a bushel. This was the same year I had harvested my one decent wheat crop, and had to sell at thirty-five cents, so I knew how he felt about that. Ever since 1931 he had been buying corn from the elevators to feed a few old milch cows, and since this feed had to be shipped in from the East, he was now paying a dollar and a half a bushel.

Next he told me about the wheat he had raised close by, and that he had been pasturing his cows on it until the fierce wind that had played such havoc with my own wheat. The gale had taken his out by the roots and scattered it far over the landscape, leaving the land bare and blowing.

"I was so sick, I couldn't eat or sleep for a week," he said; and I knew exactly how he had felt, since I had experienced the same sort of heartsickness myself. "My cows were going hungry, not because I couldn't buy feed, but because my feeling was that with everything else gone, a small item like a few old cows growing lank from hunger didn't matter one way or the other.

"But my wife gave me the dickens about that, so I went to town and bought a load of feed that set me back fifty-four bucks. That's about gone already, and if we don't pretty soon get some rain to start the weeds growing, I'll have to keep on buying feed, or else sell the cows.

"Pshaw!" he added. "If a man took a lot of machinery out into the middle of the Sahara Desert to start farming, we'd call him crazy, and probably commit him to an asylum; but, so far as I can see, we are doing exactly the same thing when we go on trying to farm in this part of the country. To my way of thinking, it is the greatest desert in the United States.

"When I bought this land and built these improvements on it, in 1929, I had quite a bit of cash on hand, and I thought I was going to make a fortune. The place set me back thirty thousand dollars, and today it isn't worth nearly as much as the six-thousand-dollar mortgage I've had to clap on it.

"Well, another year like this one, and I'll be all washed up."

This man did not tell me himself, but I have it on reliable authority that he had sunk a fortune of close to sixty thousand dollars trying to farm successfully in the Dust Bowl. He had no better fortune with his 1938 crop. Indeed, it blew out in January, and he gave up, and left the sand country for parts unknown.

When darkness fell, I left him to feed his old cows with corn at a dollar and a half a bushel, and went back to the home of his brother-in-law, who had by that time returned from his field. Except for the interesting conversation I had had, my trip proved fruitless, since, a few days before, my

friend had rented a farm on hard soil, outside of
the sand hills, and was no longer interested in a
deal on my place.

Home I went, only partly disappointed. A week
later my wheat started to recuperate. In a few
days it was looking fine, and even wheat I had
given up completely on the land that had blown so
badly began to show promise of making a crop.
There was some that was completely dead, and
when that began to move with the wind, I went to
work to list the land solid, so as to give what crop
I had left every chance to reach maturity.

Maybe the reader will begin to understand when
I speak of wheat farming in the Great Plains as a
gamble.

CHAPTER XIII

I FIGHT FOR A HARVEST

WHEN the first of May rolled around I still had five hundred acres of fine wheat, but it was beginning to burn for lack of moisture, which was another threat that I might be going to lose after all the crop I had fought so hard to save. On the eighth of May rain clouds blew up from the northwest, and I watched the storm approach, with the usual mingled hope and fear I always experienced when rain seemed about to come from that direction. As so often happened the storm split on the hogback and moved around to the southward. Where the rain fell, the thirsty land received an inch of precipitation. Mine got only a light sprinkling that was hardly enough to settle the dust on the surface of the soil. By the middle of May my crop was once again in bad shape.

Since I had not hesitated to make it known that if my 1937 crop failed I was through with farming in the Great Plains, I was not surprised to receive a visit from a farmer from near Johnson. He wanted to rent my place.

This man had been luckier than I had been. I had not had a crop since 1931, while he had had two since that year. In 1932 he had raised fifty thousand bushels of wheat, and in that much-publicized drouth year, 1934, part of his crop had shown a yield of from eight to nine bushels to the acre, at a time when he was operating two thousand acres. Since then he had run into financial difficulties. Two of his tractors had been ruined as the result of neglect, and with other machinery worn out, he had been compelled to give up part of the land he had had under control, so that now he was handling only six quarters.

With his own experience in the Dust Bowl to serve as an object lesson, I could not understand why he wanted to rent my land. Surely that experience should have told him that the occasional success of a crop here or there was no evidence that the menace of the Dust Bowl had decreased. He certainly must have known that my operations had been even less successful than his.

"This place looks like a paradise compared with where I live," he told me. "Out there the dust is moving nearly every day. Here there are a few green fields; out there there isn't any green vegetation anywhere—not even a blade of grass."

"But what good is a green field, if you cannot raise a crop?" I questioned.

"You don't have so much dust here," he insisted. "Further west, the air is filled with it every day. Even the slightest breeze starts it to fogging. There are very few farmers left where I am."

Since I was still unwilling to give up my own

struggle until my crop was hopelessly gone, he left me, disappointed by my refusal to rent my land.

Every day I scanned the sky, looking for signs of the rain that would save my wheat from ruin. One after another, neighbors saw their crops reach a condition beyond hope of salvage, but I was still in the ring when an inch of rain fell on the twenty-eighth of the month. This rain was a great relief to me, because it gave me assurance of some wheat, and when five more inches fell within a period of two weeks, I knew that I had won a partial victory in my battle with the elements. While I knew that if the rain of the eighth of May had fallen on my land, my whole acreage would have yielded a good crop, I was still thankful for what I had left; and others considered that I was to be congratulated. A weekly county newspaper publisher at Meade stated that I had the best wheat in the neighborhood, and that three quarter sections of it were estimated to yield a crop of from twenty-five to thirty bushels to the acre. This last statement was grossly exaggerated. The best wheat I had was thirty acres on one quarter that did produce thirty bushels an acre.

After the rains I worked the land which I had previously listed, where all crop had been destroyed, in order to kill the weeds and conserve the moisture in the ground. I intended to summer fallow this again. In the meantime, looking forward to the time of harvest, any work was a pleasure, since, for once, I was about to reap some return for my labors.

For the work of harvesting my grain, I engaged, well in advance, two men I knew, and the wife of one of them to keep house and prepare our meals. But as soon as we commenced the work, the first day of July, we headed into trouble, and I had to have considerable more help before my wheat was all in the bin. The wheat was so short that the header platform of the combine had to be kept dragging on the ground. Thistles that had come up since the rains in June were already high enough to be sliced off with the wheat, and they were the source of plenty of grief. My combine is as good as any on the market for threshing wheat, but it is one of the worst where weeds and thistles are mixed in with the crop. In three days of operation we broke just about every part of the machine in our attempts to make it eat these thistles along with the straw, and yet save the grain.

One of the men working for me was an old experienced hand at threshing, having owned a threshing rig before the days of the combine, but even he admitted that he was stumped. Our main trouble was that much of the stuff kept going around and around and accumulating in the returns until it would throw off, or break the chains. If this did not happen, the gears would fly off or a shaft would twist in two. My second man kept the road hot, going after repairs, and every breakdown caused some delay.

On the second day a pin holding the gear on the shaft that operated the straw walkers broke, which left the gear still on the shaft and turning. Giving all my attention to the motor, I did not immediately notice that anything was wrong, and I was adjusting the carburetor when the machine choked up. Upon investigation I found that the straw was wedged inside the machine as tight as hay in a bale, and I knew there was a hot job in store for someone, and that I was elected. The day was blistering hot, and the sun was striking directly on the thick tin over the iron framework. I well knew that the only way to free the straw was to get inside and pull it out a handful at a time. I knew that it would be like a furnace inside.

As I hesitated, building up my nerve to undertake the job, the man running my tractor volunteered: "I am a smaller man than you are. Let me crawl inside and dig it out."

I would have been glad to escape the punishment I knew was in store; but it was my rig, I was the boss, and I figured it was a job which I could not very well shirk.

Inside the machine it was fully as hot as I had anticipated. My clothes were soon wringing wet from perspiration, which, in a measure, protected my body; but every time my flesh would come in contact with the tin top or sides, the heat would

literally scorch the hide off. Nevertheless, I kept
tugging away at the straw, cussing at every breath
to keep up my morale, and, eventually I got rid of
the obstruction. When I crawled out of that inferno
after half an hour, I looked like a drowned rat
that had been scorched before drowning, and felt
even worse than that.

It was certainly a relief to have the machine
running again, but, of course, it did not last.
Within a few minutes a shaft on one of the return
augers broke, and we were stopped again.

This time I was too utterly disgusted even to try
to fix the machine. If ever I was to get my wheat
harvested, it looked as if I would have to get another combine at work in my fields. One of my
neighbors had already finished harvesting what
little crop he had, so I went over to his place, and
succeeded in hiring him to cut some of mine. Then
I went back to my own machine and found my men
working on it, which induced me to pitch in again
and help. After a while we succeeded in getting
the combine operating, and it held up until the
end of the day. But the day following, it broke in
three separate places, with resulting damage that
would require a full day to repair. The feeder-
house rattle rack would have to be taken out and
the canvas nailed down to prevent further breaking
by keeping the green thistles from the under side
of the feeder house. Incidentally, the return auger
shaft had snapped again, and the long slot keys

holding the cylinder in position on the main shaft
had been sheared off.

Exasperated at this mess, I told the men that
if they wanted to repair it they might hop right
to it, but I was through. I was ready to pull the
combine to the house and let it set there. However,
they were stout-hearted fellows, not easily discouraged, and they volunteered to fix the machine
once more; but they said if it broke again, they'd
quit too.

Part of my exasperation was due to the knowledge that time meant money, since an unfavorable
weather change might mean a heavy loss. So I
went scouting for another outfit I might hire, and
that was difficult to find. Some of the farmers still
had wheat of their own to cut, and those whose
crops had failed had not bothered to put their
combines in condition to run. However, after considerable running around, I finally located a farmer who had finished harvesting his own wheat, so
I was able to hire the outfit to help me with mine.
In a couple of hours it was in operation on my land.

With two combines at work in my fields, I
breathed more easily, and, thus encouraged, I went
back to my own machine, on which my two men
were still at work. While they went ahead repair-
ing broken parts, I gave some thought to my combine's failures, wondering if there was anything
I could do to straighten out the kinks. I knew what
I wanted that machine to do, and, even if I could

not make it do it, I did not see how I could make its performance any worse than it already was. Like a convict under death sentence making a break for liberty, I felt that I had nothing to lose, so I proceeded to make some drastic changes in the separating unit. Wonder of wonders, after the repairs were completed, the machine commenced working perfectly, with no further breaks and delays. Actually I had succeeded in ironing out its troublesome faults.

That I had succeeded in adjusting my combine to handle weedy wheat proved a life-saver, for three days later, one of the hired machines which had been encountering bigger and thicker weeds as it progressed into the field it was harvesting, was brought to a standstill, and had to quit. Sixty acres of wheat were left standing in this field, but the weeds were five feet high and a dense growth. But the wheat among these weeds was just as good as any that had been harvested from that quarter, and I could not afford to wipe it off as a loss without putting up a battle to save it. Knowing that the second hired combine was just finishing up on the field where it was working, I asked the owner to pull across the road and cut the sixty acres the other machine had abandoned, but, satisfied in advance that his machine was no better than the one that had pulled out, he refused even to make the attempt.

My own combine had still another day's cutting

to do where it was, but as soon as it had finished the field, I told my men that I was determined to get the grain from that weedy sixty acres, even if I had to get a swather to do it with, then get it from the windrows with a pick-up attachment on the combine, and thresh it after the weeds had dried. But first I tried my own machine on the weedy piece, and, much to my surprise, the remodeled combine took those tall weeds in its stride. I experienced no difficulty at all in harvesting the last of my wheat.

The year had been one constant, long-drawn-out battle, and while I was far from having a full crop, the land remaining in wheat when harvesting began averaged eleven bushels to the acre and yielded a total of six thousand bushels of grain. I sold four thousand bushels at from $1.10 to $1.16, and, after making deductions for crop rentals for land under lease, I had enough to settle my harvesting expenses. Later I had reason to wish that I had sold all my wheat at that time, but I held the balance in the bin, expecting a rise in price by September. Then I would sell for enough to enable me to put in another crop and keep going until another harvest.

CHAPTER XIV

LAST STAND

WHEREVER I went during the next two months after harvest, I was pointed out as the man who had raised far more wheat than anyone else in the locality. I might have felt like "the man who broke the bank at Monte Carlo," except that my actual net profit was negligible, and I very well knew that if I lost my next crop I would be right back where I had been before I raised this one—broke again. I don't know the fate of the Monte Carlo bank breaker, but I imagine he too went back and lost, since he, too, was a gambler.

Nevertheless, with debts paid and wheat in the bin on which I could borrow money at the bank, I found new zest in my work. My summer-fallowed land had a fine new crop of weeds, so I commenced plowing on that. As soon as it was completed, I proceeded to go over my stubble fields. Then I waited for rain. Once again I was facing the see-saw of hope and anxiety that is wheat farming in the Great Plains region; but I shall only touch the details lightly, since one year is so much like another in the Dust Bowl of today.

No rain at all fell until the first week of September. Then we had an inch that seeped into the ground far enough to meet the stored-up moisture in the subsoil on my summer-fallowed land. This I promptly drilled, and when the wheat came up, it looked very promising. But it soon showed signs of needing more moisture, and, without rain, its growth was checked.

In the latter part of September, I was becoming uneasy, because of my previous experiences with late planting, so I went ahead and drilled my stubble ground, and all the more willingly because of the fact that this land was now covered with dead weeds and thistles. Even volunteer wheat which had sprung up in the wake of our one shower early in the month had since died. Drilling through such a mass of dead vegetation would be much easier while the soil was dry. On the other hand, I knew that the cutworms would be at work on the seed as long as it lay in dry bed, so I had to gamble that rain or cold weather would come in time to check this menace.

No rain came until the middle of October, and then it was only half an inch. However, this proved enough to cause my wheat to sprout, and while the worms had feasted on quite a bit of the seed I was relieved to find that they had left enough to produce a fair crop, provided several inches of rain came before the freeze. Unfortunately for my hopes, no rain came, and, by the first of January, I knew that, in the absence of a miracle, my crop was already doomed. True, my summer-fallowed wheat was still holding its own, though two stiff gales would probably be enough to wipe it out. On my stubble ground, part of my crop was already dead, and what remained alive was sick, spindly-looking stuff that gave very little promise of survival.

In the meantime I had had to sell some of the wheat I had stored, in order to get money to settle for fuel supplies and other obligations that had accumulated since harvest. The market price, instead of rising, as I had confidently expected, had taken a drop, and I got only a dollar a bushel.

To make matters worse than they already were, the winds started early, the first one striking on the thirteenth of January, and the next on the sixteenth, and this second gale started fields to blowing. I saw very little chance of my crop's surviving, but I still had fifteen hundred bushels of wheat, and now the market had sagged to eighty cents, so I was holding on in the hope that it would go up to at least a dollar. Thus anchored to my farm for the time being, there was nothing to do but go out and make an effort to save my fields from utter ruin; and in the fore part of February, some hope was revived by a fall of rain mixed with sleet and snow. This was followed by weather unusually warm for February, and once again it looked as if I might yet harvest a fair crop. Then, in March, the winds returned to dry out the ground and start it moving again, so that, in a short time, half of my land was beyond recall, as far as the crop was concerned, and I had to ridge it up solid to save the rest.

Next came more rain, and another spell of mild weather, and what was left of my wheat soon had grown beyond the danger of blowing. Once again I felt optimistic, and all the more when more rain came in May. May was dry, and there was a period when my wheat suffered so much from lack of moisture that anxiety once more replaced hope; but, the last of the month, we had a two-inch rain followed by another two inches a few days later, and, as far as moisture was concerned, my crop was made.

This was the time I chose to dispose of the wheat I had held over in the bin, and while I got only seventy-two cents a bushel for it, as compared with the $1.16 I might have had just after the 1937 harvest, I was ready to forget this disastrous bit of speculation in the pleasure of anticipating a yield of from twenty to thirty bushels an acre from my land that still had crop.

But it was not yet harvesttime, and there was plenty of time for other calamities to strike. The first was red rust, which speedily reduced my prospects by 50 per cent. The second was a heavy rain accompanying a fifty-mile gale which struck the fifteenth of June and laid half of my wheat flat on the ground.

By the last of the month I was harvesting what

wheat was left to me. Two weeks before, I had expected a yield of from twenty to thirty bushels. Now I was getting from three to ten bushels to the acre, for a total yield of only 2500 bushels. The market price was now only sixty cents.

Once again I was faced with the old question: should I try once more or get out while I still had a shirt to my name? Again I chose to fight. I had spent considerable time and money in summer fallowing my ground. Half of it I had already worked three times, and it needed cultivating again; so I just could not see that I could quit. I worked it, then moved over on to my stubble ground; and when the third of September brought a good rain, I began drilling my summer-fallowed ground as soon as it was dry enough to permit drilling.

So much volunteer wheat came up on my stubble ground that I had to plow that once more before seeding it, but by the twentieth of September all my seed was in, and I was off to a good start for the 1939 crop stakes, when, much to my disappointment and disgust, no more moisture fell during the balance of the year. When rain did come in January, some of my crop was dead, though the major portion of it was revived. Then, the following month, the high gales returned, and naturally my crop again faced ruin. There was nothing to do but to stop the ground from moving, as I always had in the past.

Two more rains fell in March, and by the time the first of April rolled around, my wheat was a foot and a half high. This was the best wheat I had ever had out so early in the growing season, and it appeared good for thirty to forty bushels to the acre; but, as usual, the prospect soon proved to be an illusion, since no more life-giving moisture fell, and my crop burned up.

With my financial resources at last exhausted and my health seriously, if not permanently impaired, I am at last ready to admit defeat and leave the Dust Bowl forever. With youth and ambition ground into the very dust itself, I can only drift with the tide.

CHAPTER XV

EXODUS

$\mathcal{B}$*ACK* in 1930 the land was already blowing in the Dakotas, and hundreds of farmers there abandoned their farms and left their homes. In western Kansas our first experience with the black blizzards was in 1932. Coming as they did in the wake of the ruinously low prices received for the 1931 crop, these dust storms forced many farmers to leave the region to seek employment in industrial centers already overcrowded with the unemployed, or wherever they might have a friend or relative to offer aid in procuring a new start. Many of those who left in 1932 went out under doctors' orders. People who had any organic weakness could not live in the dust area.

There is just no way of arriving at accurate figures covering the number of people who have left the Great Plains in recent years, "blown out," "burned out," or "starved out." Government estimates place the migration at fifty thousand each month during the summer of 1936. Droves of them had gone before that, and they have been going by thousands ever since.

This would be reason for congratulation if they had gone to a happier lot, but thousands upon thousands of them have continued to face poverty, privation, and disease in a new environment. A great many of these refugees have gone to California, Arizona, Oregon, Washington, and Idaho. During the two and a half years between June 15, 1935, and December 31, 1937, the California Department of Agriculture counted 221,000 persons, entering the state in motor vehicles belonging to families looking for jobs at manual labor, and 84 per cent of them came from the drouth states. Sixty per cent of the people in the same classification entering Oregon, and 57 per cent of those choosing Washington have been from the same Great Plains territory, in which they could no longer eke out a living.

Numerous small towns were built up or modernized in the period between 1926 and 1930—attractive, enterprising towns with fine churches and schools. Hundreds of them are now virtually ghost towns, with homes and stores deserted and falling to decay. Half to two thirds of the population is gone. Elkhart, Kansas, once boasted a population of seventeen hundred; it has dwindled to a mere handful of some three hundred. Broken Bow, formerly a village of two hundred, had three families left the last time I was there. These are typical of hundreds of other small communities which make up the bulk of the population in the Great Plains region; and in such all-but-deserted towns anyone may take his pick of the many fine six- and eight-thousand-dollar residences built in the boom years for about one hundred dollars each.

Most farmers, when they decide to leave their farms, load their household possessions in trucks or trailers, and take to the highway under power. Many of the townspeople, having no means of transport, are forced to abandon their property and leave on foot, with only the clothes on their backs and such bundles as may be carried in their hands. After every storm the highways are thronged with these refugees. On the roads running through Meade and Montezuma I have seen hundreds of people in endless procession, heading out of the Dust Bowl. So it was in 1934, in 1935, in 1936, in 1937, and in 1938—thousands of families deserting towns and farms, all seeking some haven of relief from the dust.

Many of the farmers saved nothing even in prosperous years. Some were machine crazy, trading in used machinery on the purchase of new equipment after every crop, perhaps obtaining a trade-in credit on the basis of one third the original cost, and accepting that rather than make repairs on the machinery they had. They were determined to "keep up with the times," and demanded the benefit of every slight improvement that might make the equipment easier to handle and operate, or a little more efficient. But there were many others who, before the successive crop failures, had accumulated wealth by years of hard work and

self-denial, and were now reduced to the same
level with the improvident, the foolish, and the
vain.

Far be it from me to claim status as an authority
on the migrations of rattlesnakes, but there used
to be plenty of them in our section of the Great
Plains. Years ago a farmer showed me a gallon
bucket piled above the rim with rattles from snakes
he had killed in two years. When stock raising was
the principal industry of the plains, the cattlemen
expected to lose some stock every year from snake-
bite. Today, in our part of the country, the species
is almost extinct. I have not seen a rattler in five
years.

Black blizzards kill livestock, and small birds
trying to escape from them fall from exhaustion
and die. Human beings die too. It was estimated
that half a billion dollars worth of crops burned up
in the drouth of 1936, while sixteen hundred people
died from the effects of dust and heat.

What wonder, then, that people have been leaving the Great Plains by tens of thousands every
year. To me, that is the real tragedy of the Dust
Bowl. The Government has been doing what it
could to help with direct relief grants to needy
farmers, amounting to $49,866,446 between July 1,
1935, and June 30, 1937, plus rehabilitation loans,
most of which can never be repaid, amounting to
another $154,643,580, between April 1, 1934, and
June 30, 1937. These figures do not include allot-

ment money paid to farmers under contracts which required them to withhold a percentage of their land from crops.

In 1938 we find $10,000,000 appropriated by Congress for the fiscal year to provide loans through the Farm Security Administration to a limited number of tenants, croppers, and farm laborers for the purchase of farms. The estimate is that the appropriation will provide 2,100 loans. Contrast this with Government figures which tell us that two out of every five farmers in the United States are now tenant farmers working land which they do not own, and that the number of tenant farmers is increasing at the rate of 40,000 a year, and you have an illustration of the fact that anything the Government can do makes only a dent in a problem so vast that it staggers the intellect and even the imagination of man.

Again, compare the relief money paid out to farmers, including grants and rehabilitation loans, amounting to $204,500,000 in the period of a little over three years surveyed, with the $400,000,-000 which the Government says is lost to farmers each year, because of wind and water erosion, and you will see that as a nation we have so far been fighting a losing battle with the elements.

Perhaps I appear to be taking a pessimistic view, but that is only because everything about the Dust Bowl, I have seen published for popular consumption has ended on a note of unjustified optimism.

We are told that the Government is showing the farmers how to do it; demonstrating the advantages of contour plowing to prevent a too-speedy surface run-off; planting various crops in strips, alternating cover crops with quick cash crops; managed grazing districts with watering places for stock created with WPA labor.

These are all true, and in favored localities some of the work that is being done is going to be successful in making it possible for a few to prosper on land which the many have had to abandon in despair. At the same time, I cannot forget the many.

The Farm Security Administration has made a film called "The Plow That Broke the Plains," and has issued a "Study Guide" to be circulated with the film. Both dramatize the story of the Great Plains. The "Study Guide" states this truth: "The Federal Government cannot alone accomplish the gigantic task of making the Great Plains more liveable. Local people, directly and through their state and local governments, must take a major part."

And here is another brief quotation from the same source: "Relief to the stricken areas has made the consequences of the drouth less terrible than they might easily have been. But nothing could prevent the impoverishment of thousands of farm families, many of whom lost the farms in which they had invested all their fortunes and hopes. Nothing in the way of relief could prevent the devastation of millions of acres of land that had been stripped of its grass cover and skimmed of its top soil by the high winds."

And so the people of the Great Plains continue to leave every year, and if the numbers leaving have decreased, that is only because so many have already gone. Those who go each year are a greater percentage of the remaining population of the Dust Bowl; and the tragedy of the exodus lies in this, that these are no Argonauts setting forth in a spirit of high adventure to pioneer new frontiers, but hordes in despair, haunted by famine and disease, yet fearful of a future without hope.

Abandoned farm near Dalhart, Texas.

American gipsies: drouth refugee family on the way to California.

Many of the drouth refugees have joined the army of seasonal laborers. These have become migrant pea pickers.

Home, sweet home for the Dust Bowl refugees.

A farmer's son plays on the sand dunes that threaten to cover his home, Liberal, Kansas.

A destitute family of six camped along the roadside.

They had a home—once.

" . . . in endless procession, heading out of the Dust Bowl."

CHAPTER XVI

CONCLUSION

*A*LTHOUGH history reveals that events of major importance are likely to repeat, human beings cling to a naïve faith in the possibility of a special intervention of Providence on their personal behalf. We know that immense areas of land in central China, once cultivated valleys protected by luxuriously clad hills, are now desert, barren and dead. Excavations in the ruins of Babylon reveal to us that the now desert valley of the Euphrates was formerly a rich agricultural region supporting the earliest civilization of which we have any records. There is evidence that much of the great Sahara and Gobi deserts was once fertile. More recently, overgrazing has caused the land to blow and to destroy large areas in Australia, where entire groups of ranch buildings have been buried under drifting dirt and sand. Similarly, in Russia and Argentina, large areas are blowing. Yet, with all these examples before us, we hesitate to believe that millions of our own acres that have become affected by the same forces of destruction are permanently lost.

Government experts, however, are well aware that huge areas of the United States have been laid waste by the kind of exploitation that takes no thought of the morrow. There are numerous Government publications on the subjects of erosion, soil conservation, reclamation, and the like. The figures covering land waste are staggering. Yet, it seems to me, the great mass of the public remains indifferent, unable to grasp the immensity of the catastrophe that not only threatens, but already is upon us, as a nation.

The Government is making heroic efforts to stop the march of destruction, but, as things stand to-day, the pessimists have all the best of the argument. They hold the belief that a vast portion of the agricultural areas of the United States is fast heading towards the same fate that overtook these large areas of China and Asia Minor already referred to. One dust storm, that of May 11, 1934, is estimated to have blown 300,000,000 tons of top-soil off the great wheat plains. It took centuries of nature's methodical processes to create that valuable topsoil and place it where it would be of use to man.

The specialists tell us that 100,000,000 acres of farm land have been completely destroyed for farming at a profit; that another 125,000,000 acres are seriously damaged; and that yet another 100,000,000 acres belonging to the best farm lands are seriously threatened.

These figures are taken from a Government pamphlet published in the spring of 1936—and the land in the Great Plains region has been moving, in the blow seasons, ever since, so you may draw your own conclusions.

But consider these 1936, or, more correctly, 1935 figures. Three hundred and twenty-five million acres are going back to desert, and a lot of it is already desert. That means almost one sixth of the whole area of the United States, an area equal to all the New England states of Maine, New Hampshire, Vermont, Rhode Island, and Connecticut, plus all the mid-Atlantic states of New York, New Jersey, and Pennsylvania, plus the South Atlantic states of Delaware, Maryland, Virginia, West Virginia, North Carolina, South Carolina, Georgia, and Florida, plus the greater part of Alabama.

Stated another way, the affected areas would equal France, Germany, and all of the British Islands with the exception of Wales.

These figures apply to the whole United States, and not to the Great Plains region alone, but there are from 350,000,000 to 400,000,000 acres included in the great central strip that lies between the Mexican border and the Canadian border, and a great part of it is going, or gone.

While it is practically impossible to grasp the immensity of the figures involved or to reach even approximate accuracy, it is a fact that every black blizzard changes the figures, and invariably for the worse.

My only aim is to help the reader to understand what is taking place in the Great Plains region, and how serious it is; and, in some measure, to counteract the studied optimism of newspapers and chambers of commerce which wilfully withhold facts.

It is of the utmost importance that the truth should be widely known, for the only way the march of destruction can be halted or confined is through the adoption of better farming methods by all farmers. This ideal is impossible of attainment, except under strict regulation by wise laws adequately enforced; and to make such laws and such enforcement possible over wide stretches of our country where they are needed, an enlightened public opinion is essential. Such public opinion must recognize the sovereign right of the states and the nation to regulate the use of the land by owners and tenant farmers so that it may be conserved as a national resource.

What has become popularly known as the Dust Bowl is confined to adjacent portions of Colorado, Kansas, New Mexico, Oklahoma, and Texas. But this is misleading, so far as the lot of the farmers is concerned; and the proof of this statement is to be found in Government figures on relief grants and rehabilitation advances made in June, 1935. Considering only the Great Plains region, we find the same percentage of farmers receiving Government aid in North and South Dakota as in New

Mexico and Oklahoma; namely, 25 per cent. Colorado was in the 15 to 25 per cent bracket; Montana and Wyoming in the 10 to 15 per cent bracket; while in Texas, Kansas, and Nebraska, only 5 to 10 per cent of the farmers received relief or rehabilitation money.

Readers familiar with any particular state, or even one county, know that very different conditions may be found existing side by side, because of variations in soil and topography. Rains, or their lack, know nothing about state lines or county boundaries. But, leaving lucky spots out of the calculation, the crop failure caused by drouth in the summer of 1934 was most disastrous in the states of the Great Plains and the Rocky Mountains, and, over most of that area, amounted to over 30 per cent of all crop land, the total of crop land being figured as including what was intentionally left idle or fallow, so that the percentage of loss to crops planted was considerably higher. Moreover, the drouth of 1936, while it extended to states farther east than that of 1934, hit at its worst over the same Great Plains region; and that about finished most of us farmers. We are used to gambling with weather and markets, and most dry farmers could have survived two or three successive crop failures in the period 1934-36, if it hadn't been for previous crop failures on the one hand and the permanent aftereffects of the drouths on the other. When the high winds once started moving dirt, there was no stopping it, which I have already explained in some detail. From one farm the rich topsoil was swept clean; on the one adjoining, it might be buried under drifting dirt and sand, and there was no permanent anchorage for any of it. Millions of acres lay bare, so that even rain, when it came, helped but little. Torrents of water pulverized the dirt to a finer mesh, and washed it off the surface into the streams and gullies. Then more wind came, to blow it ten or fifteen thousand feet into the atmosphere.

Long-range forecasting is no longer highly regarded in the Dust Bowl. We recall that in the spring of 1934 a presumably noted astronomer engaged in the study of sun spots came to the conclusion that no drouth would occur in the ensuing three years. Unfortunately for his reputation as a prophet, a major drouth affected no fewer than twenty-seven states that same year, and 1936 saw another drouth even more disastrous.

But such forecasts are no less ridiculous than the theories of those optimists who hope for an end to the black blizzards on a basis of Biblical analogy —seven years of plenty and seven years of famine. This is the mirage of hope which, with Government loans and allotment payments, has kept thousands in the Dust Bowl who might have been better off from the standpoint of health, if not also financially, had they left years ago.

Equally unreliable as a foundation for optimism

are general conclusions sometimes drawn from small-scale experiments that may have been partially successful in particular localities. In the Dust Bowl area, as elsewhere, conditions vary; but, apart from this consideration, even "before and after" photographs showing, in the first a desert waste, in the second a luxuriant growing crop, are by no means conclusive. Surely, from what I have written, the reader must have learned that a good stand of crop in May or June does not by any means guarantee a successful harvest in July.

Government advisers have told the farmers to anticipate the blowing season by leaving the surface of the land rough; but dirt-laden winds chisel away at the rough surface until it, too, is pulverized to fine dust. Rough surface land, therefore, will hold only through two or three winds, and then it will be blowing like the rest. Listing is then resorted to, but listed land soon fills between the ridges, and when that happens, it begins to blow. The comparatively new damming lister which automatically closes the furrow every ten feet, to hold water from flowing down the furrows, is useful in some localities; but in regions where there is no rain in the early spring, you cannot get the lister into the dry ground. After the rains come in April and May, when we have ten to twelve inches of rainfall in two weeks, it is then too late for dam listing. If we tried it, we would lose water from the subsoil, to our net loss, since we won't receive any more rain to amount to anything during the rest of the season. The reason we work with shallow cultivation—three inches or so—is in order to kill the weeds while still holding the moisture in the ground. Then there's contour farming, which is helpful only on hilly ground where terracing is practicable, but only when rain falls at the right time.

Last year the Government offered a dollar an acre to enable farmers to plant cane on badly blown ground, on the theory that this crop, grown to six or seven feet, should then be allowed to fall and lie, to hold the ground from blowing. But after the crop had reached to a height of about two feet, with no rain coming, the hot weather cooked it, and only one wind was needed to break it right off and carry it away.

Again, some sixty miles west of me, there were favorable local rains in May and June, both in 1936 and in 1937. Hopeful farmers listed in large areas of maize, a good holding crop. It grew about a foot, or high enough to show over the tops of the ridges, but in the latter part of June and the early part of August strong winds ahead of local storms leveled the ridges into the furrows, ruining the crop and leaving the land blowing as badly as ever.

Trees were planted along the highways in Meade County in 1935. Big gasoline tanks holding five hundred to six hundred gallons, were used to water them two or three times. Most of the trees were dead in 1936, and the rest went in 1937. Even locust groves established twenty-five to thirty years ago are now dead.

Two years ago the Government took over a lot of ground in the sand country in northern Texas. With big one-hundred-horsepower tractors they cut down sand dunes twenty to thirty feet high. But the more they worked the ground, the worse it blew, until even their heavy machinery was buried and they had to give up the attempt to stop the land.

This year (1938) the Government has been paying $4 an acre for land west of me in Kansas, in eastern Colorado, and probably elsewhere. They have been able to get all they want, despite the low price; and the idea is to get it back to grass. How they are going to do it, nobody knows, but they have sold off the improvements at less than junk prices and have erected fine fences.

For my part, I am not at all convinced that large areas of land that have been once broken out and subsequently subjected to wind erosion, will ever go back to sod by the action of nature alone. If it would, the process would probably require fifteen to twenty-five years; while some say it would take fifty years. Even where the buffalo grass gets a hold in one wet year, it is speedily smothered and started to blowing with the first winds of spring. On the other hand, there is not enough seed in the country to reseed artificially any appreciable area of the Great Plains, and continue to fight successfully the destructive dirt-laden gales which continue to come year after year.

Theoretically, a farmer can keep his land from blowing by constant listing during the blowing season; but, quite apart from the fatal consequences resulting from constant work in the awful dust, the plan is impracticable. The first listing would hold the land for two or three winds, or for about a week. Then the furrows would be filled level with the ridges, with fine dust from adjoining land, or perhaps from the next county. So you split the ridges to anchor the blow dirt; and, if there is enough moisture left in the subsoil, you may even split the ridges again by listing deeper, to bring up fresh clods to hold the ground. That would be your final effort, since every time you work the land you are breaking it up more and more, and when all is dust, there is nothing more you can do to hold it.

The fact is that Government efforts, and Government-inspired measures have been constant since the land first began to blow, while an immense amount of money has been spent to aid the farmers throughout the dust area, to check their land and plant their crops. But whereas, in years previous to 1938, the Dust Bowl has extended to the foothills of the Rockies, far to the west of me, and some thirty miles to the east of me, in 1938, it is still bound by the Rockies to the west, but has extended to Pratt, Kansas, to the east, which is one hundred miles from Meade. Thus the afflicted area is more extensive than ever before.

So the spring winds, loaded with dirt, still spread their blight from field to field and from county to county; and crops that survive them live only to face the summer winds from the southwest, which, having passed over thousands of square miles of land now bare of vegetation, are surcharged with heat that cooks and destroys.

In our part of the Dust Bowl, only some five inches of topsoil is really fertile, yet I have seen fields where an oil pipe line, originally two feet underground, is exposed above the surface. There is a rock in a neighbor's field, which used occasionally to be struck by the plow, because it lay beneath the surface. That rock now stands four feet above the surface, and the land is still blowing with every wind. There are millions of acres of land in the Dust Bowl, so blown out, or so deeply buried under huge drifts of loose dirt, that it probably can never be farmed again. Even the most optimistic concede that, under the most favorable conditions that can be imagined, generations must pass before it may again be tilled profitably.

My own humble opinion is that, with the exception of a few favored localities, the whole Great Plains region is already a desert that cannot be reclaimed through the plans and labors of men.